AF507213

MYSTERY BABYLON
AND
WORLD BEASTS
UNVEILED

PETER LENGWE

Copyright © 2026 by Peter Lengwe

All rights reserved.

No part of this publication may be reproduced, distributed, or transmitted in any form or by any means, including photocopying, recording, or other electronic or mechanical methods, without the prior written permission of the publisher, except in the case of brief quotations embodied in critical reviews and certain other noncommercial uses permitted by copyright law.

All Scripture quotations are taken from the New King James Version® (NKJV).

Printed in the United States of America

ISBN:
Softcover: 978-1-972299-66-1
Hardback: 978-1-972299-67-8
eBook: 978-1-972299-65-4

For permission requests, visit and write to the publisher at:

Peter Lengwe | THE BREAD OF LIFE GLOBAL MINISTRIES

Table of Contents

PREFACE

This book was born from a deep reverence for the Word of God and a desire to understand the prophetic timeline that stretches from the Tower of Babel to the coming reign of Jesus Christ on earth.

For centuries, empires have risen and fallen—Babylon, Persia, Greece, Rome—and soon, the rise of the final beast foretold in the book of Revelation. These are not random historical shifts. They are pieces in a divine plan, allowed by God for His purposes. Each empire that ruled over Jerusalem was part of a greater prophetic pattern designed to fulfill His Word.

In the chapters that follow, I look to unveil the mystery of Babylon— not only as a literal kingdom of the past, but as a spiritual system that still influences the present world. Through the lens of Genesis, Daniel, Revelation, and other Scriptures, this work reveals how God used—even judged through—these world empires to carry out His will concerning His covenant people and His holy city.

This book is not merely historical. It is prophetic. It is theological. It is prompt. It is a call to discern the times and prepare for what lies ahead.

To every reader—whether you are a believer, a student of prophecy, or one seeking understanding—may your heart be awakened, your mind renewed, and your spirit anchored in the blessed hope of His return.

"Blessed is he who reads and those who hear the words of this prophecy..."
(Revelation 1:3, NKJV)

DEDICATION

To the One who was, and is, and is to come—

the Lord Jesus Christ, the Lamb slain from the foundation of the world.

This book is dedicated to You, my King, who opened the scroll, broke its seals, and will reign forever.

And to all believers who long for truth, watch for His appearing, and hold fast to the testimony of Jesus.

May your lamps be full, your hearts awakened, and your eyes fixed on the Author and Finisher of our faith.

INTRODUCTION: THE RISE OF REBELLION AND THE MYSTERY OF BABYLON

The name Babylon first appears in the early pages of the Bible—not as a mighty empire, but as a city called Babel, where in united pride to build a tower reaching toward heaven. It was there that God confused their language and scattered the nations.

From that moment forward, Babel, which means "confusion," became a prophetic symbol of man's rebellion against God. Though it began as a city, Babylon would rise to become one of the greatest empires in history—and beyond that, a spiritual system opposed to the Kingdom of God.

Babylon is more than ancient history. It is a mystery. A prophetic thread that weaves through Genesis, stretches across the pages of Daniel, and reaches its climactic judgment in the book of Revelation—where it is revealed as the mother of harlots and the deceiver of nations.

This book is a journey to trace that thread. From Babel to the Beast, from empires to apostasy, we will see how God allowed the kingdoms of Babylon, Persia, Greece, and Rome to rise—not by accident, but as part of His plan concerning Israel and the city of Jerusalem.

The story of Babylon is the story of man's kingdoms in defiance of God's Kingdom. It is the story of spiritual corruption, political control, and false worship masquerading as truth. But it is also a story that leads to hope—a final victory through the coming of the true King.

As you begin this journey, may the Word of God become alive in your heart. May prophecy become clear. And may you be stirred to watch, to prepare, and to worship the One who is coming soon.

Chapter 1:
The Tower of Babel and the Birth of Babylon

Confusion in the Land of Shinar

"And they said, 'Come, let us build ourselves a city, and a tower whose top is in the heavens; let us make a name for ourselves, lest we be scattered abroad over the face of the whole earth.'"
—Genesis 11:4

Babylon's origin is rooted in the soil of rebellion. Long before its name would be etched in prophetic warnings, before kings and beasts and empires rose to power, there stood a tower—a monument to mankind's pride and defiance. The city was called Babel, and it was the first great collective effort of humanity after the flood. Instead of worshipping the God who spared them, they looked to ascend by their own power.

In Hebrew, the word Babel (לְכָב) is related to the root balal (לְלְב), meaning to confuse or confound. The irony is sharp: in trying to create unity apart from God, mankind reaped divine confusion. What was meant to lift their name became a symbol of their fall. Babel was the beginning of Babylon the Great, not just in geography, but in spirit and system—a kingdom built on man's wisdom, pride, and rebellion.

The Spirit of Babylon: A Prophetic Pattern

The story of Babel is more than a historical account—it is a prophetic template. Every kingdom that would rise in opposition to God follows its pattern: unity without truth, religion without revelation, and power without submission.

In Revelation 17, Babylon called "Mystery Babylon the Great, the mother of Harlots and of the Abominations of the Earth." (Revelation 17:5). This is not merely Rome, nor only a future city, but the culmination of the rebellious system that began at Babel—a system that will be judged at the end of the age.

Daniel, centuries after Babel, saw visions of beasts—empires that would rise and fall. Yet each beast bore the DNA of that first rebellion: pride, blasphemy, and opposition to the saints of God.

Archaeological Insight: Nimrod and the Ziggurat

The Scriptures introduce Nimrod as the founder of Babel:

"The beginning of his kingdom was Babel, Erech, Accad, and Calneh, in the land of Shinar."
—Genesis 10:10

Historical and archaeological studies confirm that ancient Mesopotamia, specifically the region of Shinar, was home to some of the earliest cities. The Etemenanki, a massive ziggurat in Babylon dedicated to Marduk, is often associated with the memory of the Tower of Babel. Ancient cuneiform inscriptions describe it as "the temple of the foundation of heaven and earth." While it is a reconstruction of a later Babylonian temple, its roots may stretch back to the original ziggurat traditions from

Nimrod's time.

Archaeologists have also unearthed texts and inscriptions that speak of the confusion of languages—a rare example is a Sumerian tablet that recounts a time when all people spoke one language before the gods scattered them. Though not a direct copy of the Genesis account, it supports the biblical claim that the memory of such an event had been preserved across civilizations.

God's Judgment and the Scattering

God's response to Babel was not merely punitive—it was protective. Left unchecked, humankind would unify under a false spiritual system too soon. So, the Lord scattered them:

"Come, let Us go down and there confuse their language, that they may not understand one another's speech."
—Genesis 11:7

What God disrupted at Babel would eventually reassemble in Babylon, Assyria, Persia, and Rome—but always under divine limits. Babel's scattering delayed the rise of global tyranny until the appointed time when prophecy would unfold in full.

Jerusalem vs. Babylon: Two Cities in Conflict

From Genesis to Revelation, the Bible contrasts two cities: Babylon, the city of man, and Jerusalem, the city of God. Babel was man's attempt to reach heaven; Jerusalem is the place where God chose to come down. Babel was built by proud men; a sovereign God chose Jerusalem.

This chapter begins our journey through the empires that would arise in Babylon's shadow. We will see that every empire—Babylon, Persia, Greece, and Rome—was not only political, but spiritual. Each played a role in God's dealings with Israel and with the city of Jerusalem. And each, in its own way, reflected the spirit of Babel—confusion, pride, and resistance to the truth.

The Birthplace of Lawlessness and False Worship

The Tower of Babel was more than an act of pride—it was the seedbed of all future rebellion against God. It was here, on the plains of Shinar, that the spirit of lawlessness first manifested in full. What Satan started in the Garden— "Has God indeed said?" (Genesis 3:1)—was now taking root in the hearts of a united humanity, determined to cast off God's rule and set up a kingdom of their own.

"For the mystery of lawlessness is already at work…"
2 Thessalonians 2:7, NKJV

Paul's words reveal a spiritual reality that began long before the New Testament era. The "mystery of lawlessness" had already been at work since Babel, spreading through the nations, becoming embedded in the cultures, systems, and religions of the world. Babel was its birthplace.

The Hebrew term for lawlessness (āwen אָוֶן) implies more than just disobedience—it carries the idea of emptiness, wickedness, and idolatrous vanity. Babel was where humankind chose lawlessness over submission, autonomy over obedience.

The Origin of Idolatry and the Worship of Creation

Romans 1 speaks of humanity's descent into spiritual darkness:

"…although they knew God, they did not glorify Him as God, nor were thankful, but became futile in their thoughts… and changed the glory of the incorruptible God into an image made like corruptible man…"
Romans 1:21–23, NKJV

This passage describes exactly what happened at Babel. They rejected the Creator and exalted themselves. Instead of worshiping the God who had just judged the world by flood, they turned to the worship of created things—sun, moon, stars, animals, and eventually kings and emperors. Archaeology confirms that Babylon became the mother of all false religions, with elaborate temples, astrological practices, and pantheons of gods derived from the natural world.

In fact, ancient records describe Babel as a place where astral worship, divination, and idolatry first flourished in organized forms. Nimrod, mentioned in Genesis 10:9 as a "mighty hunter before the Lord," is believed by some early traditions to have led people away from worshiping the true God and into worship of the heavens and earthly power.

The city of Babylon would eventually be home to temples such as Esagila (dedicated to Marduk), where the ziggurat form of temple architecture gave the illusion of ascending to the heavens—a literal inversion of God's command to come down to humankind, not for man to go up by self-effort.

A Spiritual System, Not Just a City

From Babel onward, this spiritual rebellion became a system—one that would mutate into Babylon, Persia, Greece, Rome, and finally, into the Beast system of Revelation. The core of this system is still the same: reject the rule of God, exalt man, and substitute truth with deception.

Babylon is not just a city in the pages of Scripture—it is the mother of spiritual adultery (Revelation 17:5), the source of global deception, and the root of every religious system that opposes the worship of the one true God.

Setting the Stage for Prophetic Conflict

As we move into the next chapter, we will see how the Neo-Babylonian Empire under Nebuchadnezzar revived this ancient rebellion on a grand scale. With the exile of Judah, God would allow His people into the very heart of this system—not to destroy them, but to reveal His sovereignty through it.

And through a young prophet named Daniel, God would unveil visions of the kingdoms to come—empires born from the spirit of Babel, destined to rise, fall, but all shall be shattered by the stone not cut with hands (Daniel 2:34).

The Pattern Begins

As we leave the plains of Shinar and move through the Scriptures, we will trace this pattern: a city rises, a beast takes form, and God's purposes for Israel unfold. But through it all, the Word of God proves true—archaeologically, prophetically, and eternally.

In the next chapter, we will explore the rise of the Neo-Babylonian Empire under Nebuchadnezzar, and how God used Babylon as both a rod of judgment and a backdrop for some of the most detailed prophetic visions ever recorded.

CHAPTER 2: NEBUCHADNEZZAR AND THE RISE OF THE BABYLONIAN EMPIRE

Nebuchadnezzar: God's Instrument in a Pagan Throne

When we think of Babylon in the Bible, one name at once rises above the rest: Nebuchadnezzar. His power was unmatched in his time, his empire vast, and his role in Scripture unmistakable. Yet it is important to understand that Nebuchadnezzar was not the founder of Babylon, nor its first king. Babylon's origins trace back centuries to the early post-flood world, and historically, kings like Hammurabi (18th century BC) and others ruled the land long before Nebuchadnezzar's rise.

But Nebuchadnezzar was different. He was not merely a ruler of Babylon—God chose him.

"Now the rest of the people who were left in the city... Nebuzaradan the captain of the guard carried away captive to Babylon. But the poor

people… he left behind."
(2 Kings 25:11–12, NKJV)

"And now I have given all these lands into the hand of Nebuchadnezzar
the king of Babylon, My servant…"
(Jeremiah 27:6, NKJV)

That last verse is striking. God calls Nebuchadnezzar "My servant." In the Hebrew, ʿeḇeḏ (עֶבֶד), this term means slave or servant—often used for prophets or kings who carried out God's will, whether willingly or not. Though a pagan king, God used Nebuchadnezzar to execute judgment on His own people for their persistent disobedience and idolatry.

The Neo-Babylonian Empire: A Revival with a Prophetic Purpose

Babylon had existed in various forms since antiquity, but it was under Nabopolassar, Nebuchadnezzar's father, that the Neo-Babylonian Empire began to rise to global prominence around 626 BC. Nabopolassar freed Babylon from Assyrian control, and his son, Nebuchadnezzar II, would take it to unprecedented heights.

By the time Nebuchadnezzar came to power, Babylon had grown into a mighty empire, rivaling Assyria and Egypt. But while political historians may see his rise because of military strategy and statecraft, the Bible shows that it was God who raised him up for His purposes.

"The Most High rules in the kingdom of men and gives it to whomever
He chooses."
(Daniel 4:17, NKJV)

God chose nebuchadnezzar to begin the prophetic period known as "the times of the Gentiles" (Luke 21:24)—a time when Jerusalem would no longer be ruled by Davidic kings, but by Gentile powers, starting with Babylon and continuing until the return of Christ.

Jerusalem Falls: A Fulfilled Prophecy

In 605 BC, Nebuchadnezzar launched his campaign against Judah, fulfilling prophecies long spoken by Isaiah, Jeremiah, and others. The exile of Daniel and the noble captives marked the beginning of a 70-year judgment foretold by the prophet Jeremiah.

"And this whole land shall be a desolation and an astonishment, and these nations shall serve the king of Babylon seventy years."

Nebuchadnezzar did not merely conquer Judah—he became the backdrop against which God would reveal some of the most astonishing visions in Scripture. Through the exile, God positioned His faithful servant Daniel in the heart of Babylon—not to be assimilated, but to be a light in the darkness, and a mouthpiece of prophetic revelation.

The Kingdom of Gold: A Prophetic Image of Gentile Dominion

In Daniel 2, God gave Nebuchadnezzar a dream of a great image with a head of gold, chest of silver, thighs of bronze, and legs of iron. Daniel, by divine insight, revealed the meaning of the dream:

"You, O king, are a king of kings. For the God of heaven has given you a kingdom, power, strength, and glory; and wherever the children of men dwell, or the beasts of the field and the birds of the heaven, He has given them into your hand, and has made you ruler over them all—you are this head of gold."

Nebuchadnezzar's Babylon was the first of the four empires in Daniel's vision. The image stood for a succession of world kingdoms, but only one called "the head of gold." The Hebrew word for gold, zahab (בָּהָז), here is not purity, but glory, splendor, and unmatched dominion.

Yet, this golden empire would soon fall to one of silver—Medo-Persia—and the sequence would continue until the final beastly kingdom arises, far more terrifying than the rest.

A City Rebuilt on Ancient Foundations

Nebuchadnezzar is credited with rebuilding and expanding Babylon into the greatest city of the ancient world. Archaeologists have uncovered inscriptions in cuneiform, bricks stamped with his name, and records of his architectural projects—including the massive double walls, the Ishtar Gate, and what many believe to be the foundation of the fabled Hanging Gardens.

Yet the grandeur of Babylon stood in stark contrast to its spiritual emptiness. Behind the gold was a city built on rebellion. God would humble nebuchadnezzar himself—driven into madness until he acknowledged that "the Most High rules in the kingdom of men.

"And they shall drive you from men, and your dwelling shall be with the beasts of the field. They shall make you eat grass like oxen; and seven times shall pass over you, until you know that the Most High rules in the kingdom of men and gives it to whomever He chooses.""

Conclusion: The Rule of Man Under the Sovereignty of God

Nebuchadnezzar was not the first king of Babylon, but he was the first in God's prophetic timeline of Gentile dominion over Jerusalem. He was God's chosen vessel—raised up not to glorify himself, but to fulfill God's judgment, to host God's prophet, and to start the revelations that would unfold through Daniel and culminate in the Book of Revelation.

In the chapters that follow, we will examine the prophetic dreams and visions given to Daniel—visions that expose the true nature of the world's empires and point us toward the final judgment of Babylon and the return of the rightful King.

Chapter 3: The Scattering of Israel and the Empires that Ruled Them

A Chosen Nation, A Divided Kingdom

God chose Israel to be His covenant people—a kingdom of priests and a holy nation (Exodus 19:6). From the 12 sons of Jacob (whose name God changed to Israel), came the 12 tribes that made up the United Kingdom under Saul, David, and Solomon.

But after Solomon's death, the kingdom split:

- The northern kingdom became known as Israel, consisting of 10 tribes.

- The southern kingdom called Judah, consisting of the tribes of Judah and Benjamin, with some Levites.

"So, Israel has been in rebellion against the house of David to this day."
1 Kings 12:19, NKJV

This division was not just political—it was spiritual. The northern kingdom quickly fell into idolatry, rejecting the Temple in Jerusalem and setting up golden calves in Dan and Bethel (1 Kings 12:28–30). The southern kingdom remained faithful longer but eventually followed the same path.

God's Warnings Through the Prophets

God, in His mercy, sent prophets—Elijah, Hosea, Amos, Isaiah—to warn both kingdoms. But the people hardened their hearts. The result was judgment, just as foretold in the Law of Moses:

"Then the Lord will scatter you among all peoples, from one end of the earth to the other…"
Deuteronomy 28:64, NKJV

The Scattering of the Northern Kingdom (Israel) – 722 BC

In 722 BC, God allowed the Assyrian Empire under King Shalmaneser V and later Sargon II to conquer the northern kingdom of Israel.

"In the ninth year of Hoshea, the king of Assyria took Samaria and carried Israel away to Assyria…"
2 Kings 17:6, NKJV

The 10 tribes exiled and scattered throughout the Assyrian provinces:

- Halah

- Habor

- The River of Gozan

- The cities of the Medes

These Israelites are the "Lost Ten Tribes but not lost in the eyes of God." Assyria practiced forced population resettlement, mixing exiled peoples to destroy national identity. Thus, the northern tribes integrated into the nations—scattered across the ancient Near East.

The Captivity of the Southern Kingdom (Judah) – 586 BC

About 136 years later, in 586 BC, God allowed Babylon, under Nebuchadnezzar, to conquer Judah and destroy Jerusalem and the Temple.

"And the Lord gave Jehoiakim king of Judah into his hand, with some of the articles of the house of God..."
Daniel 1:2, NKJV

Judah exiled to Babylon for 70 years, as foretold by the prophet Jeremiah (25:11). Yet unlike the northern tribes, many from Judah would later return under Persian king Cyrus, rebuild the Temple, and preserve their identity—thus the name Jew comes from Judah.

Empires That Ruled Over the Scattered Tribes

Over time, various world empires ruled over the scattered tribes of Israel:

1. Assyria – scattered the northern tribes.

2. Babylon – exiled Judah.

3. Medo-Persia – allowed limited return (Ezra, Nehemiah), but still under imperial control.

4. Greece – under Alexander the Great and later Seleucid rulers (e.g., Antiochus Epiphanes).

5. Rome – occupied Israel during the time of Jesus; destroyed Jerusalem in AD 70 and again in AD 135 (Bar Kokhba revolt), scattering the Jews globally.

Where Are the Tribes Today?

Judah, Benjamin, and Levi are the tribes we can most clearly trace:

- Many Jews today descend from these three tribes, especially Judah.

- Levites (including priests or Kohanim) keep certain family traditions.

The Ten Tribes of the North remain scattered and partially unidentified:

- Some believe remnants assimilated into Jewish communities in the south before or after the Babylonian exile (2 Chronicles 30:1–11).

- Others suggest they spread as far as Africa, Asia, and Europe. Various communities—including the Beta Israel (Ethiopian Jews), Bnei Menashe (India), and others—claim descent from these tribes.

Though the exact location of every tribe is still debated, God's Word promises that He knows where they are:

"He who scattered Israel will gather him and keep him as a shepherd does his flock."
Jeremiah 31:10, NKJV

The Spiritual Significance

This scattering was not abandonment—it was discipline. God scattered Israel because of their lawlessness and idolatry, but He also promised to regather them in the last days (Ezekiel 36–37). The scattering set the stage for the times of the Gentiles—beginning with Babylon—during which Israel would be trampled underfoot by the nations until God's plan is complete (Luke 21:24).

Conclusion: A People Scattered, A Purpose Sovereign

The 12 tribes were scattered under God's judgment, but they are still part of His redemptive plan. Though hidden among the nations, their story is not lost. As we move forward into Daniel's prophetic visions, we will see how God uses Gentile empires not only to judge but to preserve, reveal, and restore.

CHAPTER 4:
NEBUCHADNEZZAR'S DREAM
OF THE IMAGE.

A Prophet in Exile, A Remnant Preserved

The fall of Jerusalem in 586 BC was not the end of God's purposes—it was the unfolding of a greater plan. Among the exiles taken to Babylon was a young man from the tribe of Judah, chosen by God not only to survive, but to become a vessel of divine revelation. His name was Daniel.

"...Daniel, Hananiah, Mishael, and Azariah were of the sons of Judah."
Daniel 1:6, NKJV

The Hebrew word for Judah is Yehudah (הָדוּהְי), meaning "praised" or "may God be praised." Though Judah had fallen into disobedience, God still preserved a faithful remnant, just as He had promised through the prophets (Isaiah 1:9; Micah 2:12). Daniel, raised in royal or noble circles, was taken into captivity as a teenager around 605 BC, during Nebuchadnezzar's first campaign against Jerusalem.

Though far from the Temple and surrounded by Babylonian idolatry, Daniel remained undefiled. His name, Daniyyel (לֹאיִנָּד), means "God is my judge." He would live true to that name in the courts of pagan kings.

The Babylonian Court and the Faith of a Young Prophet

Daniel's story opens not with visions, but with a test of loyalty. Refusing to eat the king's food or drink his wine (Daniel 1:8), Daniel and his friends chose faithfulness to God over compromise. God honored their stand, granting them wisdom, favor, and eventually, divine insight.

"As for these four young men, God gave them knowledge and skill in all literature and wisdom; and Daniel had understanding in all visions and dreams."
Daniel 1:17, NKJV

This anointing set the stage for one of the most detailed prophetic outlines in all of Scripture—visions that would stretch from Babylon to the final kingdom ruled by the beast of Revelation.

As we explore king Nebuchadnezzar's dream through the divine revelation of God to Daniel, it is important to understand that there are five kingdoms represented by five parts of the statue. Each part defined or symbolized by a metal and that each of this kingdom came in succession of each other over the rule of Jerusalem and the Israelites. It was God's own plan of judgment towards the Jews for their disobedience and lawlessness and worship of foreign gods.

"And it shall be, that just as the Lord rejoiced over you to do you good and multiply you, so the Lord will rejoice over you to destroy you and bring you to nothing; and you shall be plucked from off the land which you go to possess. "Then the Lord will scatter you among all peoples, from one end of the earth to the other, and there you shall serve other gods, which neither you nor your fathers have known—wood and stone. And among those nations you shall find no rest, nor shall the sole of your foot have a resting place; but there the Lord will give you a trembling heart, failing eyes, and anguish of soul."

"And this whole land shall be a desolation and an astonishment, and
these nations shall serve the king of Babylon seventy years. 'Then it will
come to pass, when seventy years are completed, that I will punish the king
of Babylon and that nation, the land of the Chaldeans, for their iniquity,'
says the Lord; 'and I will make it a perpetual desolation. So, I will bring
on that land all My words which I have pronounced against it, all that is
written in this book, which Jeremiah has prophesied concerning all the
nations."

DANIEL EXPLAINS THE DREAM OF NEBUCHADNEZZAR

*""You, O king, were watching; and behold, a great image! This great
image, whose splendor was excellent, stood before you; and its form
was awesome. This image's head was of fine gold, its chest and arms of
silver, its belly and thighs of bronze, its legs of iron, its feet partly of iron
and partly of clay. You watched while a stone was cut out without hands,
which struck the image on its feet of iron and clay and broke them in
pieces. Then the iron, the clay, the bronze, the silver, and the gold were
crushed together, and became like chaff from the summer threshing
floors; the wind carried them away so that no trace of them was found.
And the stone that struck the image became a great mountain and filled
the whole earth."*
Daniel 2:31-35 NKJV

DANIEL INTERPRETS THE DREAM

*"And wherever the children of men dwell, or the beasts of the field and
the birds of the heaven, He has given them into your hand and has made
you ruler over them all—you are this head of gold. But after you shall
arise another kingdom inferior to yours; then another, a third kingdom
of bronze, which shall rule over all the earth. And the fourth kingdom
shall be as strong as iron, inasmuch as iron breaks in pieces and*

shatters everything; and like iron that crushes, that kingdom will break in pieces and crush all the others. Whereas you saw the feet and toes, partly of potter's clay and partly of iron, the kingdom shall be divided; yet the strength of the iron shall be in it, just as you saw the iron mixed with ceramic clay. And as the toes of the feet were partly of iron and partly of clay, so the kingdom shall be partly strong and partly fragile. As you saw iron mixed with ceramic clay, they will mingle with the seed of men; but they will not adhere to one another, just as iron does not mix with clay."
Daniel 2:38-43 NKJV

A Dream Sent from Heaven

"You, O king, were watching; and behold, a great image! This great image, whose splendor was excellent, stood before you; and its form was awesome."
Daniel 2:31, NKJV

Nebuchadnezzar, the king of Babylon, was disturbed by a dream so vivid and overwhelming that none of his astrologers or wise men could recall or interpret it. Only Daniel, through divine revelation, was given the dream and its meaning. What Nebuchadnezzar saw was a massive statue, made of various metals—each section standing for a kingdom, and together they form a timeline of Gentile world empires that would dominate Jerusalem until the return of Messiah.

The Head of Gold – The Babylonian Empire

"This head of gold is you, O king."
Daniel 2:38, NKJV

The statue's head, made of pure gold, is Babylon, under the rule of Nebuchadnezzar. Gold was not only a symbol of wealth and majesty but also of religious power. Babylon was the first of the Gentile empires to rule over Judah and the Temple, marking the beginning of what Jesus called "the times of the Gentiles" (Luke 21:24).

The kingdom of Babylon (626–539 BC) was known for its grandeur, luxury, and spiritual corruption. Nebuchadnezzar ruled with absolute authority—his word was law. Archaeological discoveries, such as bricks stamped with his name and inscriptions from Babylon, confirm his massive building projects, including the Ishtar Gate, ziggurats, and the Hanging Gardens.

The Hebrew word for gold, zahab (זָהָב), often symbolizes glory, but in prophetic imagery, it also suggests temporary splendor without lasting foundation.

The Chest and Arms of Silver – The Medo-Persian Empire

"But after you shall arise another kingdom inferior to yours…"
Daniel 2:39, NKJV

Silver is the Medo-Persian Empire (539–331 BC), which conquered Babylon under Cyrus the Great. The two arms symbolize the dual nature of the empire—the Medes and the Persians—eventually dominated by the Persians.

Though larger in territory, this kingdom was "inferior" in centralized power. Unlike Babylon's monarchy, Persia's rule was more bureaucratic, and kings were bound by their own laws (cf. Esther 1:19). Yet God used Cyrus to fulfill prophecy by allowing the Jews to return and rebuild the Temple (Isaiah 44:28; Ezra 1:1).

Silver, in Scripture, often symbolizes redemption (Exodus 30:12–16), and indeed, under Persia, Judah experienced partial restoration.

The Belly and Thighs of Bronze – The Greek Empire

"…then another, a third kingdom of bronze, which shall rule over all the earth."
Daniel 2:39, NKJV

This third section is the Grecian Empire, set up by Alexander the Great. Bronze was a common material for armor and weapons, reflecting Greece's military prowess and swift conquest. Alexander's empire (331–323 BC) spread Greek culture (Hellenism) across the known world, deeply influencing language, philosophy, and even the Jewish world (e.g., the Septuagint translation of the Hebrew Scriptures).

After Alexander's death, his empire split into four major regions under his generals (Daniel 8:8, 11:4). The unity of Greece gave way to internal struggles—but its cultural influence persisted for centuries.

Bronze, less precious than silver or gold, speaks of strong but tarnished rule—power without the splendor of Babylon or the order of Persia.

The Legs of Iron – The Roman Empire

"And the fourth kingdom shall be as strong as iron, inasmuch as iron breaks in pieces and shatters everything..."
Daniel 2:40, NKJV

Iron is the Roman Empire (146 BC–476 AD in the West; until 1453 AD in the East). Rome was known for its brutal strength, military precision, and legal system. It crushed opposition with ruthless force. It was during the Roman occupation that Jesus was born, crucified, and the early church was set up.

The two legs may symbolize the Eastern and Western Roman Empires. Rome never fell in a day; it fractured, declined, and re-emerged in new forms throughout history.

Iron, though not as valuable as earlier metals, stands for enduring power and harsh rule. Rome left a legacy of government, roads, architecture, and persecution of God's people.

The Feet of Iron and Clay – The Final Kingdom

"Whereas you saw the feet and toes, partly of potter's clay and partly of

iron, the kingdom shall be divided…"
Daniel 2:41, NKJV

This final stage is a future kingdom—partly strong, partly fragile, made of a mixture of iron and clay. It will be divided, unstable, and internally weak despite its outward appearance of strength.

The ten toes may correlate with the ten horns in Daniel 7 and Revelation 13—a final coalition of ten kings or nations that form a revived Roman Empire. This final global order will unite political power with spiritual deception and persecution, led by the Antichrist.

Clay in Hebrew, ḥăsaf (חֲסַף), implies weakness, impermanence. The mingling of iron and clay suggests incompatibility—a divided kingdom forced together, politically united but ideologically or culturally fractured.

The Stone Cut Without Hands – The Coming of Christ

"And in the days of these kings the God of heaven will set up a kingdom which shall never be destroyed…"
Daniel 2:44, NKJV

This final part of the dream climaxes with a stone "cut without hands"—a supernatural force that shatters the statue entirely. This is not a man-made kingdom, but the Messianic Kingdom of Jesus Christ, which will crush every human empire and fill the whole earth with righteousness.

This stone becomes a majestic mountain—a common biblical image of God's government (Isaiah 2:2–4; Micah 4:1).

Conclusion: The Image Stands, But Not Forever

Nebuchadnezzar saw the entire scope of Gentile dominion over Jerusalem—from Babylon to the future world order. Each metal stood for a real kingdom with a prophetic role. Yet they all shared one trait: they would fall.

Only the kingdom set up by the Stone of God will endure.

In the next chapter, we will explore Daniel's vision of the four beasts, which reveals the true spiritual nature of these kingdoms, and how their final form will arise to oppose the saints—only to be destroyed at the return of the King.

It is important to note that there are five parts of the statue symbolized by five types of metals, therefore standing for five kingdoms and not four kingdoms as many theologians and Christians have understood. Let us look at the five parts and the metals and five kingdoms.

FIVE PARTS	FIVE METALS	FIVE KINGDOMS IN SUCCESSION
HEARD	GOLD	BABYLON EMPIRE
CHEST/ARMS	SILVER	MEDO-PERSIA EMPIRE
BELLY/THIGHS	BRONZE	GREEK EMPIRE
LEGS	IRON	ROMAN EMPIRE
FEET	IRON/CLAY	OTTOMAN/ MOHAMMEDAN POWER

As you can see these kingdoms exist in succession over the rule of Jerusalem, it is of utmost importance to know and understand the mind of God. Ever prophecy in the book of Daniel has to do with Jerusalem and God's people the Jews and how God used the pagan kingdoms to bring judgment to the Jews. Another important fact to know is that these empires are only reckoned in succession when they came in possession of Jerusalem, it does not mean they never existed. Interesting when you look at the interpretation of the dream by the prophet Daniel, he uses ordinal numberings as in first, second, third, fourth to describe the succession the empires power over Jerusalem. As you can see from the above diagram, I have listed the empires in their succession, but the fifth one is the one needing explanation.

"Whereas you saw the feet and toes, partly of potter's clay and partly of iron, the kingdom shall be divided; yet the strength of the iron shall

be in it, just as you saw the iron mixed with ceramic clay. And as the toes of the feet were partly of iron and partly of clay, so the kingdom shall be partly strong and partly fragile. As you saw iron mixed with ceramic clay, they will mingle with the seed of men; but they will not adhere to one another, just as iron does not mix with clay. And in the days of these kings the God of heaven will set up a kingdom which shall never be destroyed; and the kingdom shall not be left to other people; it shall break in pieces and consume all these kingdoms, and it shall stand forever."
Daniel 2:41-44 NKJV

This fifth empire is revealed in the vv,41-44. The power that took possession of Jerusalem after the Roman Empire was the mohammedan power of Egypt part of the Ottoman Empire. This empire though not mentioned in the Bible by name was referred to by our Lord Jesus in the gospel of Luke.

"And they will fall by the edge of the sword, and be led away captive into all nations. And Jerusalem will be trampled by Gentiles until the times of the Gentiles are fulfilled."
Luke 21:24 NKJV

After the destruction of Jerusalem by the Romans in 70AD, the period of the gentiles (Mohammedan power) began just as the Lord Jesus Christ prophesied and indeed Jerusalem was trampled. The word trampled means to tread under foot, trampled on, ie.to treat with insult and contempt: to desecrate the Holy things in this case the Holy city Jerusalem. This desecration of Jerusalem happened when the Muslim region took over the Holy site on the mount olive where the original temple was built and there, they built their temple which is an abomination in the site of God.

This fifth power is described in v.21as the feet and toes, it took possession of Jerusalem from the battle of Actium in 31B.C- A.D 636. As you can see its characteristic is described by the feet, Jerusalem was indeed trodden down until the year 1947 when Israel became independent.

The other description of the fifth empire is the toes, as you are aware that humans have ten toes, these ten toes are ten nations that shall rise in the end times. So, this fifth empire takes us all the way to the beast of revelation 13. This is why I love to study the word of God; it is intriguing like a puzzle. You must connect pieces together to see the full picture.

"Then I stood on the sand of the sea. And I saw a beast rising out of the sea, having seven heads and ten horns, and on his horns ten crowns, and on his heads a blasphemous name."
Revelation 13:1 NKJV

"And another sign appeared in heaven: behold, a great, fiery red dragon having seven heads and ten horns, and seven diadems on his heads."
Revelation 12:3 NKJV

As you see in both scriptures, I have provided from the book of revelation, ten horns are the ten toes of the book of Daniel. These ten toes or ten horn are ten nations that shall rise in the end times and will be part of the beast (the Antichrist). The ten nations will be made up of some European nations and Arab nations

Daniel 2:42-43 describe the make up of these ten nations partly (European nations) and partly clay (Arab nations) and partly strong (European nations) and partly brittle i.e, easily broken or fragile (Arab nations) and v.43 adds that these nations will not mix in marriage and mingle or cling to one another just as the iron do not mix clay.

Then the book of revelation tells us what will happen at the time of the ten nations in the end times to fulfill Daniel 2:44.

""The ten horns which you saw are ten kings who have received no kingdom as yet, but they receive authority for one hour as kings with the beast. These are of one mind, and they will give their power and authority to the beast. These will make war with the Lamb, and the Lamb will overcome them, for He is Lord of Lords and King of kings;

and those who are with Him are called, chosen, and faithful.""
Revelation 17:12-14 NKJV

*"And in the days of these kings the God of heaven will set up a kingdom
which shall never be destroyed; and the kingdom shall not be left to
other people; it shall break in pieces and consume all these kingdoms,
and it shall stand forever."*
Daniel 2:44 NKJV

The puzzle is solved!

Chapter 5:
Daniel's first vision:
The Loin, the Bear, the Leopard, and the little horn

"Daniel spoke, saying, "I saw in my vision by night, and behold, the four winds of heaven were stirring up the Great Sea. And four great beasts came up from the sea, each different from the other. The first was like a lion and had eagle's wings. I watched till its wings were plucked off; and it was lifted up from the earth and made to stand on two feet like a man, and a man's heart was given to it. "And suddenly another beast, a second, like a bear. It was raised up on one side and had three ribs in its mouth between its teeth. And they said thus to it: 'Arise, devour much flesh!' "After this I looked, and there was another, like a leopard, which had on its back four wings of a bird. The beast also had four heads, and dominion was given to it. "After this I saw in the night visions, and behold, a fourth beast, dreadful and terrible, exceedingly strong. It had

huge iron teeth; it was devouring, breaking in pieces, and trampling the residue with its feet. It was different from all the beasts that were before it, and it had ten horns. I was considering the horns, and there was another horn, a little one, coming up among them, before whom three of the first horns were plucked out by the roots. And there, in this horn, were eyes like the eyes of a man, and a mouth speaking pompous words."
Daniel 7:2-8 NKJV

The definition of the word beast as used in the bible is that of a man whose aspect is of a wild animal with irrational impulse and acting instinctively driven by evil spirit. These four beasts are seen coming up from the sea by Daniel differing from those in the dream of Nebuchadnezzar. These beasts will co-exist at some point in time, and they do not come in succession as those beast Daniel 2, and they do not appear to have any contact or rule over Jerusalem but will be part of the end time beast of revelation 13. After much study I have concluded that the first three beasts are 21st century empires but the fourth has not yet been established because it is the beast of revelation 13, the beast of the Antichrist.

"Then I stood on the sand of the sea. And I saw a beast rising up out of the sea, having seven heads and ten horns, and on his horns ten crowns, and on his heads a blasphemous name. Now the beast which I saw was like a leopard, his feet were like the feet of a bear, and his mouth like the mouth of a lion. The dragon gave him his power, his throne, and great authority."
Revelation 13:1-2 NKJV

Revelation 13 proves my point. The only beast from Nebuchadnezzar's dream in Daniel 2 connected to the end time beast of revelation 13 is the ten toes which are the ten horns.

Now let us look at the four beasts of Daniel's vision.

"I saw in my vision by night, and behold, the four winds of heaven were

stirring up the Great Sea. And four great beasts came up from the sea,
each different from the other."
Daniel 7:2–3, NKJV

Daniel's vision, recorded in the first year of Belshazzar's reign, king Belshazzar was king Nebuchadnezzar's grand son who took over the Babylon empire after the death of king Nebuchadnezzar. So, from this information we can deduce that the kingdom of Babylon was still in power. Daniel would have not seen it coming up because it was already in existence and in power when he had the vision of the four beasts. this proves my point of view.

The "Great Sea" biblically refers to the Mediterranean Sea, prophetically it means the restlessness of nations or the instability in the world (cf. Revelation 17:15). The "four winds" stirring the sea symbolize global turmoil—wars, revolutions, and divine judgment—out of which arise four terrifying world powers.

The First Three Beasts: A Present-Day Perspective

While traditional interpretation sees these four beasts as parallel to the four kingdoms of Daniel 2, this chapter presents a prophetic alternative: the first three beasts are distinct, symbolic of contemporary national powers, with only the fourth beast aligning directly with the empire of the end.

The Lion with Eagle's Wings – Possibly England and the U.S.

"The first was like a lion and had eagle's wings. I watched till its wings
were plucked off; and it was lifted up from the earth and made to stand
on two feet like a man, and a man's heart was given to it."
Daniel 7:4, NKJV

The lion has long been the emblem of the British Empire. The eagle's wings, symbolic of swiftness and reach, could be the United States, which historically emerged from Britain. The plucking of the wings may indicate the separation of these powers, and the transformation into a standing

"man" with a human heart may reflect a political or ideological shift—
toward humanitarianism or liberalism over imperialism.

The Bear Raised on One Side – Possibly Russia

*"And suddenly another beast, a second, like a bear. It was raised up on
one side, and had three ribs in its mouth between its teeth..."*
Daniel 7:5, NKJV

The bear is a common symbol for Russia, especially in modern
geopolitics. The imagery of it being "raised up on one side" suggests an
imbalance or asymmetric power, as seen in Russia's internal structure or
post-Soviet dominance. The three ribs may be past or future conquests—
the Baltic States, Crimea, or other regions. The command to "devour much
flesh" implies future aggression.

The Leopard with Four Wings and Four Heads – Possibly Germany or Another Global Force

*"After this I looked, and there was another, like a leopard, which had on
its back four wings... and the beast also had four heads, and dominion
was given to it."*
Daniel 7:6, NKJV

The leopard implies speed, adaptability, and deadly precision. It
could be a nation like Germany, known for its engineering, militarism,
and efficiency, especially during WWII. The four wings and four heads
suggest both rapid conquest and multiple spheres of control, a coalition
or federation rather than a single ruler.

The Fourth Beast – The Final Empire of the Antichrist

*"After this I saw in the night visions, and behold, a fourth beast,
dreadful and terrible, exceedingly strong. It had huge iron teeth; it was
devouring, breaking in pieces... It was different from all the beasts that
were before it, and it had ten horns."*
Daniel 7:7, NKJV

This beast is unlike anything that came before. It is not likened to any known animal—it is unnatural, terrifying, and prophetically unique. This is the revived Roman Empire, the final one-world government under the leadership of the Antichrist. It is technocratic, military, economic, and spiritual tyranny combined, and it had ten horns which are the ten toes of king Nebuchadnezzar's dream.

The ten horns are ten king that will rule under this empire. From among them rises the "little horn," who grows in power, speaks blasphemies, and makes war against the saints (Daniel 7:8, 21).

"I was considering the horns, and there was another horn, a little one, coming up among them... In this horn, were eyes like the eyes of a man, and a mouth speaking pompous words."
Daniel 7:8, NKJV

This little horn is the Antichrist—politically astute, spiritually deceptive, and violently opposed to the Kingdom of God. He is going to rise at the time of unsettling in the Middle East, and he will be seen as the answer to the peace in the Middle east between Israel and the Arab nations and he is of the ten horns which means he is Arabic... (Saudi king)? I am just saying let us be watchful because he will be the main player in bringing the Arab nations to the table to sign the seven years pace agreement between Israel and the Arab nations and part of the agreement will be the building of the final temple at the Temple Mount olive. These things are just unfolding right in our very eyes.

The Judgment of the Beasts

"The court was seated, and the books were opened..."
Daniel 7:10, NKJV

Daniel then sees a heavenly court convened. The Ancient of Days (God the Father) sits in judgment. Thrones are set. Fire proceeds from Him. Judgment is passed—not just on the fourth beast, but on the entire system of rebellious kingdoms. The beast is slain, and its body destroyed.

The others lose their dominion but are allowed to remain "for a season and a time" (Daniel 7:12).

The Son of Man Receives the Kingdom

"Then to Him was given dominion and glory and a kingdom…"
Daniel 7:14, NKJV

This glorious moment introduces the Messiah—Jesus Christ—as the One to whom the Father gives everlasting dominion. The phrase "Son of Man" is directly used by Jesus of Himself (Matthew 24:30; Mark 14:62), linking this prophecy to His second coming.

In Greek, the word for dominion in the New Testament, kratos (κράτος), implies mighty strength and ruling power. This will be the final kingdom, never to be replaced or corrupted.

Conclusion: The Rise of the Final Beast and the Fall of Man's Kingdoms

Daniel's vision reveals the true nature of world powers—animalistic, brutal, and temporary. Though the first three beasts may already exist today as national powers, the fourth is yet to arise in full—the final one-world empire, empowered by Satan, led by the Antichrist, and prophesied to make war with the saints.

But his rule will be short. The Ancient of Days has already set the time of judgment. And the Kingdom of the Son will fill the earth.

CHAPTER 6:
DANIEL'S SECOND VISION:
THE RAM, THE MALE GOAT,
AND THE LITTLE HORN

"I saw in the vision, and it so happened while I was looking, that I was in Shushan, the citadel, which is in the province of Elam; and I saw in the vision that I was by the River Ulai. Then I lifted my eyes and saw, and there, standing beside the river, was a ram which had two horns, and the two horns were high; but one was higher than the other, and the higher one came up last. I saw the ram pushing westward, northward, and southward, so that no animal could withstand him; nor was there any that could deliver from his hand, but he did according to his will and became great. And as I was considering, suddenly a male goat came from the west, across the surface of the whole earth, without touching the ground; and the goat had a notable horn between his eyes. Then he came to the ram that had two horns, which I had seen standing beside the river, and ran at him with furious power. And I saw him confronting the ram; he was moved with rage against him, attacked the ram, and

broke his two horns. There was no power in the ram to withstand him, but he cast him down to the ground and trampled him; and there was no one that could deliver the ram from his hand. Therefore, the male goat grew very great; but when he became strong, the large horn was broken, and in place of it four notable ones came up toward the four winds of heaven. And out of one of them came a little horn which grew exceedingly great toward the south, toward the east, and toward the Glorious Land."
Daniel 8:2-9 NKJV

A Vision by the River: Divine Clarity and Prophetic Detail

"Then I lifted my eyes and saw, and there, standing beside the river, was a ram which had two horns…"
Daniel 8:3, NKJV

Two years after the vision of the four beasts (Daniel 7), Daniel received another vision—this time in Shushan, in the province of Elam, by the river Ulai. This vision did not repeat the symbols of Daniel 7 (modern beasts) but instead introduced a ram and a male goat—each clearly showed by the angel Gabriel as real, historic empires.

Unlike Daniel 7, which holds mystery and symbolic ambiguity, Daniel 8 is direct and confirmed by the text itself as a continuation of Nebuchadnezzar's dream. Here, the metals of the statue in Daniel 2— silver and bronze—correspond to the ram and the goat.

"The ram which you saw, having the two horns—they are the kings of Media and Persia. And the male goat is the kingdom of Greece."
Daniel 8:20–21, NKJV

This clarity leaves no doubt: Daniel 8 carries forward Nebuchadnezzar's dream—not in symbolic imagery of modern nations, but in prophetic detail about historical world empires.

The Ram with Two Horns – Medo-Persian Empire (The Chest and Arms of Silver)

"I saw the ram pushing westward, northward, and southward, so that no animal could withstand him..."
Daniel 8:4, NKJV

The ram had two horns, being the dual power of the Medes and the Persians. The higher horn came up last representing the rise of Persia as the dominant force. This perfectly aligns with the chest and arms of silver from Nebuchadnezzar's statue (Daniel 2:32).

Medo-Persia expanded rapidly across the known world—westward toward Lydia and Asia Minor, northward toward Armenia, and southward into Egypt. No beast (empire) could stand before it.

As Gabriel explicitly told Daniel:

"The ram which you saw... they are the kings of Media and Persia."
(Daniel 8:20, NKJV

This removes all speculation—this empire is the same as the second kingdom in Nebuchadnezzar's dream, confirming Daniel 8 as the true continuation.

The Male Goat with the Notable Horn – The Greek Empire (The Belly and Thighs of Bronze)

"Then as I was considering, suddenly a male goat came from the west... and the goat had a notable horn between his eyes."
Daniel 8:5, NKJV

The male goat is Greece, and the notable horn is none other than Alexander the Great. The goat moved swiftly—without touching the ground—reflecting Alexander's rapid conquests across Persia, Egypt, and into India in just over a decade.

"The male goat is the kingdom of Greece. The large horn... is the first king."
Daniel 8:21, NKJV

This aligns with the belly and thighs of bronze in the statue of Daniel 2—being the Greek Empire that followed Persia.

Alexander's sudden death led to the fulfillment of the next part of the vision:

"And the large horn was broken, and in place of it four notable ones came up..."
Daniel 8:8, NKJV

After Alexander's death in 323 BC, his empire split among four generals:

1. Cassander – Macedonia and Greece

2. Lysimachus – Thrace and Asia Minor

3. Seleucus – Syria and Mesopotamia

4. Ptolemy – Egypt

These four divisions are represented by the four horns—a prophetic detail unparalleled in historical precision.

The Little Horn – A Foreshadowing of Antichrist

"And out of one of them came a little horn which grew exceedingly great..."
Daniel 8:9, NKJV

From the Seleucid division arose Antiochus IV Epiphanes, a king who persecuted the Jews, desecrated the Temple, and foreshadowed the actions of the final Antichrist.

"He even exalted himself as high as the Prince of the host... and by him

the daily sacrifices were taken away..."
Daniel 8:11, NKJV

Antiochus desecrated the Temple by sacrificing a pig on the altar and setting up an idol of Zeus—an event commemorated in the Jewish festival of Hanukkah. This is a type of the "abomination of desolation" that Jesus later warned would happen again in the future (Matthew 24:15).

Thus, Daniel 8 not only confirms the identity of past empires but also prefigures the final world leader who will arise in the spirit of Antiochus—the Antichrist.

How This Vision Connects with Nebuchadnezzar's Dream

To summarize:

Daniel 2 (Statue)	Daniel 8 (Vision)	Kingdom
Chest & arms of silver	Ram with two horns	Medo-Persia
Belly & thighs of bronze	Goat with notable horn	Greece
Not represented here	Little horn from four horns	Antiochus (type of Antichrist)

Daniel 8 does not include Babylon because the vision was given during the Babylonian Empire, and it had already been represented as the head of gold. It also does not include Rome because I believe the little horn of the first vision of Daniel 7:7 will be a personification or the rebirth of the Roman Empire in union with the the iron/clay (the feet and the toes ie.the ten nations) and the three modern beasts, the lion, and, the bear and, the leopard. This is the beast of the end times (revelation 13) that is why this beast will be terrifying and of fierce countenance. Therefore, Daniel 8 fills in the middle layers of Nebuchadnezzar's statue in precise detail.

"I was considering the horns, and there was another horn, a little one, coming up among them, before whom three of the first horns were plucked out by the roots. And there, in this horn, were eyes like the eyes of a man, and a mouth speaking pompous words."

"And out of one of them came a little horn which grew exceedingly great toward the south, toward the east, and toward the Glorious Land."
Daniel 8:9 NKJV

Conclusion: Prophecy Fulfilled and Yet to Be Fulfilled

Daniel 8 is not a symbolic mystery, but a divine unveiling of history in advance. It proves that the statue in Daniel 2 was not a myth or poetic metaphor—it was a prophetic timeline, now partially fulfilled. Now from the two visions of Daniel 7and 8 the focus will shift to Daniel's people, the Jew's, servitude, in exile and the restoration of the beloved city of God, Jerusalem and the rebuilding of the temple of God. Then before the end of the book of Daniel the focus will turn back to the coming of the little horn (revelation 13) and how God will judge the Jews and destroy the little horn's empire. But there is a gap between the book of Daniel and the book of revelation, this bridge period consists of the birth of the promised messiah (Christ Jesus), His suffering, death, resurrections, and ascendancy then the birth of His body (The church) which will take us all the way to the book of revelation to fulfill Daniel's prophecy. So, hang tight with me as we journey through the Holy scriptures.

Conclusion: Prophecy Fulfilled and Yet to Be Fulfilled

CHAPTER 7:
THE SEVENTY-YEAR SERVITUDE AND GOD'S REDEMPTIVE TIMELINE

Why Seventy Years? A Divine Judgment Rooted in Covenant

"And this whole land shall be a desolation and an astonishment, and these nations shall serve the king of Babylon seventy years."
Jeremiah 25:11, NKJV

The 70-year exile was not a random number—it was a divinely measured judgment rooted in Israel's repeated violation of God's covenant. To understand the prophecy of Daniel, we must first understand the justice of God in determining the number 70.

The Violation of the Land Sabbaths

"Then the land shall enjoy its sabbaths as long as it lies desolate... as

long as it lies desolate it shall rest—for the time it did not rest on your
sabbaths when you dwelt in it."
Leviticus 26:34–35, NKJV

God commanded Israel to allow the land to rest every seventh year—a Sabbath year (see Leviticus 25). But for 490 years, Israel had ignored this law. Instead of resting the land, they pursued gain, disregarded God's commands, and oppressed the poor.

According to 2 Chronicles 36:21, the 70-year exile fulfilled the number of Sabbaths the land had missed:

"To fulfill the word of the Lord by the mouth of Jeremiah, until the land had enjoyed her Sabbaths. If she lay desolate, she kept Sabbath, to fulfill seventy years."

So, 490 years of disobedience resulted in 70 years of enforced rest—a one-for-seven judgment. God was not only judging Israel for idolatry but also restoring righteousness to the land.

The Curse of the Covenant

Israel's exile was also the fulfillment of the covenant warnings in Deuteronomy 28 and Leviticus 26. If Israel disobeyed, God warned He would:

- Remove them from the land (Lev. 26:33)

- Scatter them among the nations (Deut. 28:64)

- Cause their land to become desolate (Lev. 26:32)

God was not acting unjustly. He was fulfilling His covenant—both its blessings and its curses. This exile became a turning point in Israel's national identity and a trigger for the prophetic visions that would follow.

Daniel's Realization in Babylon

"I, Daniel, understood by the books the number of the years… that He would accomplish seventy years in the desolations of Jerusalem."
Daniel 9:2, NKJV

Daniel, still in exile and in his 80s, realized through reading Jeremiah's scroll that the 70 years of judgment were complete. But instead of demanding deliverance, he repents on behalf of the nation (Daniel 9:3–19).

God responds not only by confirming the 70 years—but by giving Daniel a far greater timeline: 70 weeks of years (490 years). Just as 490 years of disobedience led to 70 years of captivity, another 490-year plan would unfold—this time centered on Messiah and final redemption.

God's Justice and Mercy in Perfect Balance

The 70 years of servitude were not merely punishment—they were prophetic correction. God was cleansing the land, fulfilling His covenant, and setting the prophetic clock for everything that follows—including the birth of the Messiah, the Church Age, the rise of the final beast, and the return of Christ.

In the next section of this chapter, we will explore how the 70 weeks of Daniel 9 extend from this first judgment and carry us into the very heart of the book of Revelation.

The Seventy Weeks – Prophetic Timeline to Messiah and the End:

From Seventy Years to Seventy Weeks

In response to Daniel's intercession and understanding of the seventy years, God gave him a broader vision—not just of past judgment, but of future redemption.

"At the beginning of your supplications the command went out, and I have come to tell you, for you are greatly beloved; therefore consider the matter, and understand the vision: "Seventy weeks are determined

For your people and for your holy city, To finish the transgression, To make an end of sins, To make reconciliation for iniquity, To bring in everlasting righteousness, To seal up vision and prophecy, And to anoint the Most Holy."
Daniel 9:23-24 NKJV

The word translated "weeks" is the Hebrew שָׁבֻעַ (shavu 'a), meaning a unit of seven. In this context, it refers to seventy sets of seven years—a total of 490 prophetic years. This is God's comprehensive timeline for dealing with:

- Israel's sin

- The coming of the Messiah

- The establishment of everlasting righteousness

- The final judgment

The Breakdown of the 70 Weeks

""Know therefore and understand, that from the going forth of the command to restore and build Jerusalem Until Messiah the Prince, there shall be seven weeks and sixty-two weeks; The street shall be built again, and the wall, even in troublesome times."
Daniel 9:25 NKJV

Let us break it down:

- 7 weeks (49 years) – Time to rebuild Jerusalem (fulfilled after the decree of Artaxerxes in 457 BC).

- 62 weeks (434 years) – Time from the rebuilding to the coming of Messiah.

  - Combined, this is 69 weeks, or 483 years.

  - 1 week (7 years) – The final week, which is yet future.

""And after the sixty-two weeks Messiah shall be cut off, but not for Himself; And the people of the prince who is to come Shall destroy the city and the sanctuary. The end of it shall be with a flood, and till the end of the war desolations are determined."
Daniel 9:26 NKJV

This is a direct prophecy of the crucifixion of Jesus Christ. The Hebrew word for "cut off" is תָּרֵכ (karath), used for covenant sacrifice—Jesus was cut off not for Himself, but for our sins (Isaiah 53:8).

The Prophetic Gap – From Messiah's Death to the Final Week

After the 69th week (the coming and crucifixion of the Messiah), there is a pause in the prophetic timeline—a gap that the Old Testament prophets could not fully see: the Church Age.

"Searching what, or what manner of time, the Spirit of Christ who was in them was indicating when He testified beforehand the sufferings of Christ and the glories that would follow."
I Peter 1:11 NKJV

"…and the people of the prince who is to come shall destroy the city and the sanctuary."
Daniel 9:26, NKJV

"For days will come upon you when your enemies will build an embankment around you, surround you and close you in on every side, and level you, and your children within you, to the ground; and they will not leave in you one stone upon another, because you did not know the time of your visitation.""
Luke 19:43-44 NKJV

This was fulfilled in 70 AD, when the Romans destroyed Jerusalem and the Temple—just as Jesus prophesied. But this destruction did not fulfill the final week. That 70th week is yet future.

The Church Age, called a mystery by Paul is the time when the gospel is preached to all nations, and the body of Christ is formed—a people made up of both Jew and Gentile.

"By which, when you read, you may understand my knowledge in the mystery of Christ), which in other ages was not made known to the sons of men, as it has now been revealed by the Spirit to His holy apostles and prophets:"
Ephesians 3:4-5 NKJV

The Final Week – The 7-Year Tribulation

"Then he shall confirm a covenant with many for one week; But in the middle of the week, He shall bring an end to sacrifice and offering. And on the wing of abominations shall be one who makes desolate, even until the consummation, which is determined, is poured out on the desolate.""
Daniel 9:27 NKJV

This refers to the little horn (the Antichrist), the "prince who is to come." He will make a 7-year covenant or treaty with Israel, and the ten nations but will break it halfway through, committing the abomination of desolation (cf. Matthew 24:15).

This final week is the Tribulation, the same seven-year period detailed in Revelation chapters 6–19. It is the fulfillment of the final 70th week of Daniel's prophecy.

The Connection to Revelation

Daniel's prophecy ends with the kingdom of man in rebellion and the people of God awaiting deliverance. Revelation picks up where Daniel ends:

- The Antichrist (Daniel's "little horn") appears in Revelation 13.

- The 10 kings of Daniel 7 appear in Revelation 17.

- The abomination of desolation in Daniel 9 appears in Revelation 11 and 13.

- The judgment of the beast and the establishment of Christ's eternal kingdom (Daniel 7:14) is fulfilled in Revelation 19–20.

"Blessed is he who waits and comes to the one thousand three hundred and thirty-five days."
(Daniel 12:12, NKJV)

This links with Revelation's timeline of 1,260 days (3.5 years), confirming a shared prophetic framework.

Conclusion: One Prophetic Timeline, One Sovereign God

God's prophetic clock began with Israel's 70 years of servitude. It expanded to 490 years with the vision of the 70 weeks. 69 of those weeks have been fulfilled, but one final week remains. Between the 69th and 70th week stands the cross, the resurrection, and the Church.

We now wait for the final events—the rise of the final beast, the time of Jacob's trouble, and the coming of the Son of Man in glory.

CHAPTER 8:
THE MYSTERY OF THE CHURCH AND THE ONE TRUE FAITH

The word "church" in our English Bibles is not a direct translation of the original Greek. The word used in the New Testament is ἐκκλησία (ekklēsía), which means "a called-out assembly" or "gathering of people summoned for a purpose."

- Ek (ἐκ) = "out of"

- Kaleō (καλέω) = "to call"

So, the Church is not a building or institution—it is a body of people called out of the world and into Christ.

The English word church comes from the Old English cirice, which was derived from the Greek kuriakos, meaning "belonging to the Lord" (kuriakē oikia = the Lord's house). Over time, this term was applied to physical buildings, but that shift in meaning obscured the original concept of the Church as a living body of believers, not a location or religious organization.

This linguistic change has contributed to centuries of misunderstanding. Many associate "church" with a place, a denomination, or a hierarchical system. But in Scripture, the ἐκκλησία refers to:

- A local assembly of believers (Acts 14:27)

- The universal body of Christ (Ephesians 1:22–23)

- Those spiritually reborn through the gospel (Romans 1:6–7)

"For by one Spirit we were all baptized into one body—whether Jews or Greeks, whether slaves or free—and have all been made to drink into one Spirit."
1 Corinthians 12:13, NKJV

This means the true Church is:

- Invisible in identity but visible in fruit

- Spiritual in nature, not political or cultural

- Christ's body on earth, with Him as the Head (Colossians 1:18)

Why This Matters Prophetically

Understanding that the Church is a spiritual body, not an earthly institution, helps make sense of why it is absent in Revelation 4–19. The focus returns to Israel and the nations during the Tribulation—not the Church. The ἐκκλησία is called out to be a witness, a bride, and a people for His name—and its mission will be complete before the final week of Daniel's prophecy.

A Mystery Kept Hidden for Ages

"...the mystery which in other ages was not made known to the sons of

The Church—the body of Christ made up of both Jews and Gentiles—was not revealed to the Old Testament prophets. Though glimpses of God's plan for the nations appear in Isaiah, Psalms, and other prophetic writings, the existence, nature, and function of the Church stayed a divine mystery, hidden until after the resurrection of Jesus Christ.

The Greek word used for "mystery" is μυστήριον (mystērion), meaning a truth once hidden, but now divinely revealed. In the context of Ephesians, it refers specifically to God's plan to create one new man from Jew and Gentile through Christ (Ephesians 2:14–16).

The Apostle Paul: Steward of the Mystery

"To me... this grace was given, that I should preach among the Gentiles the unsearchable riches of Christ, and to make all see what is the fellowship of the mystery...”
Ephesians 3:8–9, NKJV

Paul was entrusted with the stewardship (oikonomia) of this mystery. The Church is not a replacement for Israel, but a separate and unique body created through the blood of Christ, formed by the indwelling of the Holy Spirit, and tasked with declaring God's wisdom to the world and even to the heavenly hosts (Ephesians 3:10).

The prophets saw the mountain peaks of Messiah's suffering and His kingdom, but they did not see the valley in between—the Church Age.

Why the Mystery Was Kept Hidden

God concealed the Church for a purpose:

1. To fulfill the redemptive plan without interference: Had Satan known what the death of Christ would accomplish—creating a Spirit-filled body that would carry His presence globally—he

might not have instigated the crucifixion (1 Corinthians 2:7–8).

2. To unify all things in Christ: The Church would be the tool through which God would begin reconciling all things in heaven and earth (Ephesians 1:10).

3. To prevent the premature fulfillment of prophecy: The hidden nature of the Church preserved the prophetic timeline, keeping the focus on Israel until the appointed time.

The True Church: Not a Denomination, But a Body

The true Church is not a building, institution, or denomination—it is a living, spiritual body united by faith in Jesus Christ.

"For by one Spirit we were all baptized into one body—whether Jews or Greeks..."
1 Corinthians 12:13, NKJV

Characteristics of the true Church:

• It is built on the foundation of Christ (Ephesians 2:20).

• It is in-dwelt by the Holy Spirit (Ephesians 1:13–14).

• It is composed of born-again believers, not just attendees or members.

• It is called to holiness, unity, and the Great Commission.

Jesus said, "I will build My Church, and the gates of Hades shall not prevail against it" (Matthew 16:18). This promise was not made to any one local congregation or religious system, but to the global, Spirit-born body of believers united in Him.

The Role of the Church in the Last Days

The Church is not the beast, not Babylon, and not Israel. It is the light in the darkness, the salt of the earth, and the bride waiting for the

Bridegroom.

During the prophetic gap between Daniel's 69th and 70th weeks:

- The Church is proclaiming the gospel.

- It is being purified and tested.

- It awaits the rapture and return of Christ (1 Thessalonians 4:16–17).

But once the 70th week begins—the seven-year Tribulation—the prophetic spotlight returns to Israel and the nations, not the Church.

The Mystery Now Made Known

The mystery hidden for ages has now been revealed. The Church is not a replacement for Israel, but a new creation in Christ, formed from every tribe, tongue, and nation. Understanding this mystery helps us see why Daniel's timeline paused, why Revelation resumes it, and why the final beast cannot rise until the Church's mission is complete.

The True Foundation of the Church – One Faith, One Lord, One Salvation

"For no other foundation can anyone lay than that which is laid, which is Jesus Christ."
1 Corinthians 3:11, NKJV

A denomination, a council, or a pope did not found the Church. The true Church was founded by Jesus Christ Himself, who said:

"I will build My church, and the gates of Hades shall not prevail against it."
Matthew 16:18, NKJV

The foundation of the Church is not Peter, nor Paul, nor any man—but Christ crucified and risen.

"...on this rock I will build My church..."
(Matthew 16:18)—that "rock" is the confession Peter made:

"You are the Christ, the Son of the living God." (v. 16)

Salvation by Grace Alone, Through Faith Alone, in Christ Alone

"For by grace you have been saved through faith, and that not of yourselves; it is the gift of God, not of works, lest anyone should boast."
Ephesians 2:8–9, NKJV

The Church is made up of people who are:

- Saved by grace, not by works, religion, or heritage.

- Born again, not just baptized into a tradition.

- Redeemed by the blood of Jesus, not by their own merit.

This is what separates the true Church from all other belief systems and religious communities—even those that may seem "Christian" on the surface. Only the Church founded on the gospel of grace through faith in the crucified and risen Christ has the promise of eternal life.

The Exclusivity of Christ – One Way only and No Other Way!

"Jesus said to him, 'I am the way, the truth, and the life. No one comes to the Father except through Me.'"
John 14:6, NKJV

This is not arrogance—it is truth from the mouth of the One who rose from the dead. The true Church boldly confesses:

- There is one God—the Creator of heaven and earth.

- There is one Mediator—Jesus Christ, fully God and fully man.

- There is one gospel—the death, burial, and resurrection of Jesus for the forgiveness of sins.

Other beliefs may acknowledge Jesus as a prophet, moral teacher, or founder—but only the true Church worships Him as the eternal Son of God, crucified for our sins and raised for our justification.

"Nor is there salvation in any other, for there is no other name under heaven given among men by which we must be saved."
Acts 4:12, NKJV

A Loving Warning to Other Believers

To any reader who holds to a different faith, tradition, or religious background: This truth is not shared to condemn, but to invite. God does not delight in the death of the wicked (Ezekiel 33:11), but desires that all should come to repentance (2 Peter 3:9). The true Church is not an exclusive club—it is a global call to repent and believe the gospel.

We are saved not by rituals, laws, or the faith of our ancestors—but by trusting in the finished work of Jesus Christ on the cross. He alone bore our sin. He alone conquered death. He alone gives eternal life.

The Church's Identity and Destiny

- We are His body (1 Corinthians 12:27).

- We are His bride (Revelation 19:7).

- We are His witnesses (Acts 1:8).

- We are His temple (Ephesians 2:21–22).

- We are His inheritance (Ephesians 1:18).

The true Church is the only entity on earth that has been redeemed by the blood of Jesus (Acts 20:28), and the only group that will be snatched up to meet Him in the air. 1 Thessalonians 4:16–17

The One True Church, The One Living God

The Church is not one of many paths to God. It is the only path God Himself established—through His Son, Jesus Christ. It is a mystery once hidden, now revealed, and it is open to all who will believe.

Baptism by Immersion – A True Picture of the Gospel

One of the clear and consistent practices of the early Church was baptism by full immersion in water, not by sprinkling or pouring. This practice was not a religious ritual or tradition—it was a powerful, symbolic act that expressed faith in the death, burial, and resurrection of Jesus Christ.

"Therefore, we were buried with Him through baptism into death, that just as Christ was raised from the dead by the glory of the Father, even so we also should walk in newness of life."
Romans 6:4, NKJV

The Greek word used in the New Testament for baptism is βαπτίζω (baptizō), which means:

- To immerse

- To submerge

- To dip beneath

There is no biblical support for baptism by sprinkling infants or adults. The apostles and the early Church consistently baptized believers by immersion after their profession of faith in Jesus Christ.

"Both Philip and the eunuch went down into the water, and he baptized him."
Acts 8:38, NKJV

This was the normative pattern:

1. Hear the gospel.

2.   Believe in the Lord Jesus Christ.

3.   Be baptized by immersion as a public confession of faith.

Why Immersion Matters

Immersion is not just about getting wet. It visually and spiritually portrays:

- Death to the old life (going under the water).

- Burial with Christ (being submerged).

- Resurrection to new life (coming up out of the water).

Sprinkling, while common in many traditions, does not communicate this biblical symbolism, nor is it practiced anywhere in the New Testament.

"He who believes and is baptized will be saved; but he who does not believe will be condemned."
Mark 16:16, NKJV

While baptism does not save by itself, it is the commanded and immediate response of saving faith (Acts 2:38). It is the first step of obedience in the life of a true disciple of Christ.

Not for Infants, But for Believers

There is no biblical command or example of infant baptism. Baptism follows personal belief in the gospel. A baby cannot repent, believe, or confess Jesus as Lord. Only a believer can be baptized in the way Scripture teaches.

Conclusion: A Mark of the True Church

The true Church does not baptize for tradition—it baptizes to obey Christ. The method matters because truth matters. Baptism by immersion in the name of the Father, the Son, and the Holy Spirit is:

- A testimony of faith.

- A symbol of spiritual transformation.

- A step of obedience every true disciple takes.

Baptized in One Spirit – A Complete Work of the Triune God

"For by one Spirit we were all baptized into one body—whether Jews or Greeks, whether slaves or free—and have all been made to drink into one Spirit."
1 Corinthians 12:13, NKJV

Biblical baptism reflects more than an outward act of obedience—it signifies a spiritual reality: that all true believers are baptized by the Holy Spirit into the body of Christ, under the authority of the Father.

This baptism affirms the complete work of the Triune God in salvation:

The Father

– Planned salvation from before the foundation of the world.

"Blessed be the God and Father… who chose us in Him before the foundation of the world…"
Ephesians 1:3–4 NKJV

The Son

– Accomplished salvation through His death and resurrection.

"…having made peace through the blood of His cross…"
Colossians 1:20 NKJV

The Holy Spirit

– Applies salvation by regenerating, sealing, and baptizing

the believer into Christ.

"...by one Spirit we were all baptized into one body..."
1 Corinthians 12:13

The Name of the Trinity in Water Baptism

Jesus Himself commanded that baptism be carried out in the name of the Father, and of the Son, and of the Holy Spirit:

"Go therefore and make disciples of all the nations, baptizing them in the name of the Father and of the Son and of the Holy Spirit..."
Matthew 28:19, NKJV

Notice that the word is "name" (singular), not "names." This emphasizes that God is one, yet three in person. To be baptized in the name of the Trinity is to be fully identified with the one true God.

Trinitarian Unity in the Church

Just as the Trinity is one, so the true Church is called to unity in:

- One Lord (Jesus Christ),

- One faith (the gospel),

- One baptism (spiritual and symbolic),

- One Spirit (who dwells in all believers),

- One God and Father of all.

"There is one body and one Spirit... one Lord, one faith, one baptism: one God and Father of all..."
Ephesians 4:4–6, NKJV

Baptism, both in water and in Spirit, is a public declaration and inward transformation that reflects the complete work of the triune God in every true believer. I will let the true and Holy word of God to speak for itself and may it be the light to your feet. I love my God and my Lord Jesus Christ.

""Hear, O Israel: The Lord our God, the Lord is one!"
Deuteronomy 6:4 NKJV

"I am the Lord, and there is no other; There is no God besides Me. I will gird you, though you have not known Me,"
Isaiah 45:5 NKJV

"Yet for us there is one God, the Father, of whom are all things, and we for Him; and one Lord Jesus Christ, through whom are all things, and through whom we live."
I Corinthians 8:6 NKJV

""O Lord of hosts, God of Israel, the One who dwells between the cherubim, you are God, You alone, of all the kingdoms of the earth. You have made heaven and earth."
Isaiah 37:16 NKJV

"For who is God, except the Lord? And who is a rock, except our God?"
Psalms 18:31 NKJV

"Therefore, I make known to you that no one speaking by the Spirit of God calls Jesus accursed, and no one can say that Jesus is Lord except by the Holy Spirit. There are diversities of gifts, but the same Spirit. There are differences of ministries, but the same Lord. And there are diversities of activities, but it is the same God who works all in all. But the manifestation of the Spirit is given to each one for the profit of all: for to one is given the word of wisdom through the Spirit, to another the word of knowledge through the same Spirit, to another faith by the same Spirit, to another gifts of healings by the same Spirit, to another the working of miracles, to another prophecy, to another discerning of spirits, to another different kinds of tongues, to another the interpretation of tongues."
I Corinthians 12:3-10 NKJV

Chapter 9:
The True Church God vs. Mystery Babylon the Prostitute

1. The True Church – Born of the Spirit at Pentecost

"And when the Day of Pentecost had fully come… they were all filled
with the Holy Spirit…"
Acts 2:1,4, NKJV

The Church that Jesus promised to build (Matthew 16:18) was birthed on the Day of Pentecost, not by councils or emperors, but by the outpouring of the Holy Spirit. This Church:

- Proclaimed the gospel of Jesus Christ crucified and risen.

- Was led by apostles and elders, not by popes or political rulers.

- Met in homes and open gatherings, not ornate temples.

- Preached salvation by grace through faith, not through sacraments or works.

"And the Lord added to the church daily those who were being saved."
Acts 2:47, NKJV

This is the true Church—a body of believers united by faith in Christ and the indwelling Holy Spirit.

2. The Rise of a Different Church – Political Power and Doctrinal Corruption

As time passed, a different entity began to appear:

- Rooted in Rome, not Jerusalem.

- Founded on imperial authority, not apostolic teaching.

- Wielding political and military power, not spiritual truth.

By the 4th century, under Emperor Constantine, Christianity was institutionalized. What had begun as a Spirit-led movement became an imperial religion.

- Pagan practices were mixed with Christian symbols.

- Bishops gained civil power.

- The seat of authority shifted from Christ to men.

"They profess to know God, but in works they deny Him…"
Titus 1:16, NKJV

This is not the Church Jesus founded.

3. The Roman Catholic Church – A Religious-Political Hybrid

Many traditions upheld by the Roman Catholic Church are not rooted in Scripture, but in human tradition and pagan assimilation:

- The worship of Mary as "Queen of Heaven" (cf. Jeremiah 7:18)

- Prayers to the dead (forbidden in Deuteronomy 18:10–11)

- Papal infallibility and titles like "Vicar of Christ"

- Use of idols, relics, incense, and ritual that mirrors ancient Babylon

The Catholic Church became not only a religion, but a kingdom, with its own:

- Government

- Currency

- Military alliances

- Claim to rule over kings and nations

"With whom the kings of the earth committed fornication, and the inhabitants of the earth were made drunk with the wine of her fornication."
Revelation 17:2, NKJV

This fits the prophetic description of Mystery Babylon—a spiritual harlot who rides the beast of world power.

4. Mystery Babylon – The Great Harlot of Revelation 17

"And I saw a woman sitting on a scarlet beast... arrayed in purple and scarlet, and adorned with gold and precious stones and pearls... and on her forehead a name was written MYSTERY, BABYLON THE GREAT, THE MOTHER OF HARLOTS..."
Revelation 17:3–5, NKJV

The parallels are striking:

- Purple and scarlet – the colors of Catholic hierarchy.

- Drunk with the blood of saints – think of the Inquisitions and martyrdoms.

- Sits on seven hills – Rome is famously known as the "City on Seven Hills" (Revelation 17:9).

- A global influence – she reigns over "the kings of the earth" (Rev. 17:18).

This system masquerades as the Church but is a counterfeit that leads many astray.

5. The Final Warning and Call to Come Out

"Come out of her, my people, lest you share in her sins, and lest you receive of her plagues."
Revelation 18:4, NKJV

God is not against Catholics as individuals—He loves them. But He is against the system that has blasphemed His name, corrupted His gospel, and aligned with world powers in the name of religion.

To any Catholic reader, or anyone deceived by religious tradition: this is a call to return to the Word of God, to repent, and to believe in the true gospel of grace through faith in Christ alone.

Two Churches – One True, One False

- One is born at Pentecost, the other at the seat of empire.

- One is led by the Holy Spirit, the other by worldly power.

- One proclaims Christ alone; the other adds tradition.

- One is the Bride of Christ; the other is the Harlot of Babylon.

The Leadership of the True Church – According to

God's Word

"And He Himself gave some to be apostles, some prophets, some evangelists, and some pastors and teachers..."
Ephesians 4:11, NKJV

The Church of God is led by Spirit-appointed, Scripture-defined offices—not by religious hierarchy, titles of supremacy, or political control. According to the New Testament, Jesus set up a fivefold ministry for the building up of His body:

➤

Apostles

– Sent ones who lay foundations and set up churches (Eph. 2:20)

➤

Prophets

– Those who speak God's Word and edify the Church

➤

Evangelists

– Preachers of the gospel to the lost

➤

Pastors

– Shepherds who care for and oversee local flocks

➤

Teachers

– Instructors grounded in the Word, guiding with sound

doctrine

These are spiritual roles, not priestly offices. Nowhere in the New Testament are believers told to set up priests, cardinals, or a pope as head over the Church.

No Priests, No "Holy Father" – One Mediator, One Lord

"For there is one God and one Mediator between God and men, the Man Christ Jesus…"
1 Timothy 2:5, NKJV

The idea of a separate priesthood ruling over believers is not New Testament doctrine—it is a return to the Old Covenant, which Christ fulfilled.

In the true Church:

Every believer is a priest in Christ (1 Peter 2:9)

No one is to be called "Father" in a spiritual sense

"Do not call anyone on earth your father; for One is your Father, He who is in heaven."
Matthew 23:9, NKJV

The title "Holy Father" is reserved for God alone. Yet the Roman Catholic Church assigns this title to the pope, claiming divine authority on earth. This is not biblical—it is blasphemous.

Future Kingdom Priests – At Christ's Return, Not Before

"And has made us kings and priests to His God and Father, to Him be glory and dominion forever and ever. Amen."
Revelation 1:6, NKJV

The true priesthood of believers is fulfilled when Jesus returns and sets up His kingdom. We are now being prepared, but we are not yet reigning. The Roman system tries to reign before the time, exalting men to priesthood and kingship prematurely.

> *"Do you not know that the saints will judge the world?"*
> *1 Corinthians 6:2, NKJV*

That authority belongs to resurrected and glorified saints—not popes or priests in the present age.

Conclusion of This Section

The true Church is led by the Spirit and the Word, not by hierarchy and religious tradition. Titles like "Holy Father," "Pontiff," or "Vicar of Christ" do not come from Christ, but from Babylonian religious imitation.

Only one is our High Priest—Jesus Christ (Hebrews 4:14).

Only one is our Holy Father—God in heaven.

Only one will make us kingdom priests—the Lamb who was slain (Revelation 5:10).

Biblical Aspect	Mystery Babylon	Roman Catholic Church
Name Given in Revelation	Mystery, Babylon the Great, the mother of Harlots	Calls itself 'Holy Mother Church'
Colors Worn (Rev. 17:4)	Purple and Scarlet	Bishops/Cardinals wear purple & scarlet
Golden Cup (Rev. 17:4)	Golden cup full of abominations	Golden chalices used in Mass
Drunk with the Blood of Saints (Rev. 17:6)	Yes	Responsible for inquisitions & martyrdoms
Sits on Seven Hills (Rev. 17:9)	Yes	Rome is known as the City on Seven Hills
Mother of Harlots (Rev. 17:5)	Yes	Claims to be the mother church
Reigns over Kings of the Earth (Rev. 17:18)	Yes	Historically influenced kings and governments
Blasphemous Titles (Rev. 13:6)	Yes	Uses titles like 'Holy Father', 'Vicar of Christ'

| Adorns with Gold and Jewels (Rev. 17:4) | Yes | Vatican treasures include gold and precious stones |
| Commits Fornication with Kings (Rev. 17:2) | Yes | Has longstanding political alliances with nations |

Two Women in Revelation – The Harlot vs. The Bride

Aspect	Mystery Babylon – The Harlot	The Bride of Christ – New Jerusalem
Revelation Chapters	Revelation 17–18	Revelation 19–21
Symbolizes	False religion, corrupt church	The true Church, purified bride
Clothed in	Purple, scarlet, adorned with gold and pearls (Rev. 17:4)	Fine linen, clean and white (Rev. 19:8)
Name Given	Mystery, Babylon the Great, Mother of Harlots (Rev. 17:5)	The Lamb's wife, the Holy City (Rev. 21:9–10)
Dwelling	Sits on many waters and seven hills (Rev. 17:1, 9)	Comes down from heaven, from God (Rev. 21:2)
Relationship to Kings	Commits fornication with kings of the earth (Rev. 17:2)	Married to the King of Kings (Rev. 19:7)
Spiritual Condition	Drunk with the blood of saints and martyrs (Rev. 17:6)	Holy, without spot or wrinkle (Eph. 5:27)
Destiny	Judged, burned, and destroyed (Rev. 18:8–10)	Reigns forever with Christ (Rev. 22:5)
Source of Glory	Earthly wealth, human power	God's glory and the Lamb (Rev. 21:23)

A Call to Choose: The Woman You Follow Reveals the Faith You Profess

One woman deceives the nations and leads to judgment.

The other is prepared for her Husband and enters eternal glory.

"Come out of her, my people, lest you share in her sins, and lest you receive of her plagues."
Revelation 18:4, NKJV

"Let us be glad and rejoice and give Him glory, for the marriage of the Lamb has come, and His wife has made herself ready."
Revelation 19:7, NKJV NKJV

This comparison underscores what is at stake: to be part of the true Church, one must be redeemed by Christ, separated from spiritual corruption, and awaiting the return of the Bridegroom.

Chapter 10:
The Rise of the Little Horn – From Daniel to Revelation

DANIEL'S VISION OF THE LITTLE HORN IN CHAPTER SEVEN

""After this I saw in the night visions, and behold, a fourth beast, dreadful and terrible, exceedingly strong. It had huge iron teeth; it was devouring, breaking in pieces, and trampling the residue with its feet. It was different from all the beasts that were before it, and it had ten horns. I was considering the horns, and there was another horn, a little one, coming up among them, before whom three of the first horns were plucked out by the roots. And there, in this horn, were eyes like the eyes of a man, and a mouth speaking pompous words."
Daniel 7:8 NKJV

""Then I wished to know the truth about the fourth beast, which was

different from all the others, exceedingly dreadful, with its teeth of iron and its nails of bronze, which devoured, broke in pieces, and trampled the residue with its feet; and the ten horns that were on its head, and the other horn which came up, before which three fell, namely, that horn which had eyes and a mouth which spoke pompous words, whose appearance was greater than his fellows."
Daniel 7:19-20 NKJV

GABRIEL INTERPRETATION OF THE DANIEL'S VISION

""Thus, he said: 'The fourth beast shall be A fourth kingdom on earth, which shall be different from all other kingdoms, and shall devour the whole earth, trample it, and break it in pieces. The ten horns are ten kings Who shall arise from this kingdom. And another shall rise after them; He shall be different from the first ones and shall subdue three kings. He shall speak pompous words against the Most High, shall persecute the saints of the Most High, and shall intend to change times and law. Then the saints shall be given into his hand for a time and times and half a time."
Daniel 7:23-25 NKJV

DANIEL'S VISION OF THE LITTLE HORN IN CHAPTER EIGHT

"And out of one of them came a little horn which grew exceedingly great toward the south, toward the east, and toward the Glorious Land. And it grew up to the host of heaven; and it cast down some of the host and some of the stars to the ground and trampled them. He even exalted himself as high as the Prince of the host; and by him the daily sacrifices were taken away, and the place of His sanctuary was cast down. Because of transgression, an army was given over to the horn to oppose the daily sacrifices; and he cast truth down to the ground. He did all this and prospered."
Daniel 8:9-12 NKJV

GABRIEL INTERPRETS DANIEL'S SECOND VISION

"Then it happened, when I, Daniel, had seen the vision and was seeking the meaning, that suddenly there stood before me one having the appearance of a man. And I heard a man's voice between the banks of the Ulai, who called, and said, "Gabriel, make this man understand the vision." So, he came near where I stood, and when he came, I was afraid and fell on my face; but he said to me, "Understand, son of man, that the vision refers to the time of the end." Now, as he was speaking with me, I was in a deep sleep with my face to the ground; but he touched me and stood me upright. And he said, "Look, I am making known to you what shall happen in the latter time of the indignation; for at the appointed time the end shall be."
Daniel 8:15-19 NKJV

""And in the latter time of their kingdom, When the transgressors have reached their fullness, A king shall arise, having fierce features, who understands sinister schemes. His power shall be mighty, but not by his own power; He shall destroy fearfully and shall prosper and thrive; He shall destroy the mighty, and also the holy people. "Through his cunning He shall cause deceit to prosper under his rule; And he shall exalt himself in his heart. He shall destroy many in their prosperity. He shall even rise against the Prince of princes; But he shall be broken without human means. "And the vision of the evenings and mornings Which was told is true; Therefore, seal up the vision, for it refers to many days in the future.""
Daniel 8:23-26 NKJV

From the time of Daniel's exile in Babylon to the terrifying visions he received of future empires and beasts, God began to unveil a prophetic warning—a ruler who would arise, fierce in countenance and empowered by Satan himself. This "little horn" is the future beast of revelation 13. He will arise to fulfill the last seven years of the seventy years servitude of the Jews and the city of Jerusalem.

This chapter traces the rise of the little horn from Daniel's visions and their interpretation by Gabriel which needs no interpretation by anybody. These visions of the little horn are one and as Gabriel says, for it refers to many days in the future which takes us to the end times.

In the first vision in Daniel 7 the little horn is seen rising among the existing four modern powers. The fourth being the most dreadful and terrible exceedingly strong and had huge iron teeth. This fourth beast is not the Roman Empire but the end times world empire of revelation 13 which has some characteristics of the Roman Empire but more dreadful and diverse like any other empires before it and it has ten horns, and the little horn will rise among the ten horns (Nations). This beast of of revelation 13 will co-exist with the three beasts the lion, the bear, and the leopard but because of its strength it will pluck out the lion, the bear, and the leopard by their roots

"I was considering the horns, and there was another horn, a little one, coming up among them…"
Daniel 7:8 NKJV

And in the second vision Daniel 8, which takes us back to the beasts that succeeded the Babylonian empire of king Nebuchadnezzar. The Ram which is the medo-Persia empire that succeeded the Babylon empire and then the Greek empire that succeeded the media-Persia empire and from Greek empire, four kingdoms rise after the death of Alexander the greet. From these four kingdoms comes the little horn, so the little horn will be a direct descendant of one of the four kings. Interestingly Daniel is not shown the Roman Empire that succeeded the Greek empire as if foreseeing the Roman Empire as a shadow of the beast of the end times which will have the iron strength.

This horn is:

- Intelligent and boastful – "a mouth speaking pompous words"

- Blasphemous – opposing the Most High

- Aggressive – making war with the saints and prevailing

- Revolutionary – looking to change times and laws

- Temporary – ruling for "a time, times, and half a time" (3½ years)

This figure is not merely symbolic. He is prophetically tied to a final ruler, described with even more detail in the last book of the Bible.

The Beast of Revelation – The Manifestation of the Little Horn

"Then I stood on the sand of the sea. And I saw a beast rising up out of the sea, having seven heads and ten horns…"
Revelation 13:1, NKJV

This beast from the sea is the full-grown form of Daniel's little horn. He arises from the nations (the sea) and is empowered by the dragon (Satan).

He:

- Blasphemes God and His tabernacle

- Makes war against the saints and overcomes them

- Exercises global authority for 42 months (3½ years)

- Demands universal worship

- Establishes a global economic system tied to a mark—666

The parallels to Daniel's vision are exact. The beast is the little horn revealed, now empowered by Satan and ruling over a united global kingdom of rebellion.

Antichrist Spirit Throughout History – Foreshadows of the Beast

The apostle John reminds us that the spirit of Antichrist is already at work:

"Even now many antichrists have come, by which we know that it is the last hour."
1 John 2:18 NKJV

While the final Antichrist is yet to be revealed, history has been filled with precursors—figures who embodied his rebellion, deception, and persecution of God's people. These are prophetic "types"—shadows pointing to the beast to come.

Foreshadows of the Antichrist:

Name	Traits Matching the Antichrist
Nimrod (Genesis 10–11)	First tyrant; built Babel; opposed God
Pharaoh (Exodus)	Hardened heart; enslaved God's people; defied God's Word
Antiochus Epiphanes (Daniel 8)	Desecrated temple; exalted himself as god; persecuted Jews
Roman Caesars	Claimed divinity; martyred Christians; global dominance
Mohammad	Denied Jesus' divinity; claimed new revelation; warred against Jews and Christians
Popes and Inquisitors	Usurped spiritual authority; persecuted saints; claimed infallibility
Hitler	Antisemitic genocide; charismatic control; inspired by occult powers

Each of these carried the spirit of Antichrist, but none fully fulfilled the prophecies of Daniel and Revelation. They were forerunners—preparing the world for the final deception.

CHAPTER 11:
DANIEL'S PROPHETIC TIMELINES

"And he said to me, 'For two thousand three hundred days; then the
sanctuary shall be cleansed.'"
Daniel 8:14, NKJV

One of the most astounding demonstrations of God's sovereignty over history is found in the prophetic time periods revealed in the book of Daniel. These time markers, stretching across centuries, are not random—they are intricately designed to align with the unfolding of prophetic events in the book of Revelation.

Daniel was not just given visions of beasts and kingdoms—he was given prophetic numbers that mark the timeline of Israel's future, the rise of the Antichrist, and the return of the Messiah. These periods also act as prophetic keys, linking the Old and New Testament apocalyptic texts.

In this chapter, we will examine six prophetic periods of time from the book of Daniel and align them with their parallels in the book of Revelation.

1. The Seventy Weeks

""Seventy weeks are determined for your people and for your holy
city, to finish the transgression, to make an end of sins, to make
reconciliation for iniquity, to bring in everlasting righteousness, to seal
up vision and prophecy, and to anoint the Most Holy. "Know therefore
and understand, that from the going forth of the command to restore and
build Jerusalem Until Messiah the Prince, there shall be seven weeks
and sixty-two weeks; The street shall be built again, and the wall, even
in troublesome times. "And after the sixty-two weeks Messiah shall be
cut off, but not for Himself; And the people of the prince who is to come
Shall destroy the city and the sanctuary. The end of it shall be with a
flood, and till the end of the war desolations are determined. Then he
shall confirm a covenant with many for one week; But in the middle of
the week, He shall bring an end to sacrifice and offering. And on the
wing of abominations shall be one who makes desolate, even until the
consummation, which is determined, is poured out on the desolate. ""
Daniel 9:24-27 NKJV

The seventy "weeks" represent seventy sets of seven years, totaling 490 prophetic years. These are divided into three distinct phases:

- 7 weeks (49 years) – the rebuilding of Jerusalem

- 62 weeks (434 years) – leading up to the coming of the Messiah

- 1 week (7 years) – a final future period of covenant and betrayal

At the end of the 69 weeks, the Messiah is "cut off", a clear prophecy of Christ's crucifixion. But not for Himself i.e, He shall be rejected and crucified and His same kingdom He came to now is in abeyance. And the people (the Romans) of the prince (the little horn) that shall come shall destroy the city and the sanctuary; this was fulfilled in 70AD but now we await the little horn's time the seven remaining years to complete the whole 70 years prophecy. V.26 continues to say and till the end of the war desolation are determined, I.e, looking forward to the end of the seven years right after the three and half years of the great tribulation desolation are determined.i. e, desolate places (Matthew 23:38).

V.27 takes us back to the beginning of the seven years and marks the beginning of the last seven years. Then he (the little horn, the Antichrist) shall confirm (to act insolently) a covenant (a treaty or a pledge) with many (the ten nations included) for one week (seven years) to seek for peace in the Middle East. What remains is the 70th week—the Tribulation period. In the middle of this week (3½ years in), the Antichrist breaks his covenant and sets up the abomination of desolation.

Revelation Parallel:

The 70th week perfectly aligns with the seven-year tribulation, split into two halves—each 3½ years. The second half is the Great Tribulation, vividly described in Revelation 6–19.

2. Time, Times, and Half a Time

"Then the saints shall be given into his hand for a time and times and half a time."
Daniel 7:25 NKJV

This phrase refers to:

- Time (1 year)

- Times (2 years)

- Half a time (½ year)

Total: 3½ years

This is the period during which the Antichrist persecutes the saints, opposes God, and dominates the earth.

Revelation Parallel:

- 42 months (Revelation 13:5)

- 1,260 days (Revelation 11:3; 12:6)

- Time, times, and half a time (Revelation 12:14)

Each of these confirms the same 3½ year span of intense tribulation and satanic rule.

3. The 1,260 Days (Daniel & Revelation)

This number appears in both books:

"And the woman fled into the wilderness… 1,260 days."
Revelation 12:6 NKJV

- Symbolizes the time God preserves Israel (or the faithful remnant) during persecution

- Equivalent to 42 months, or 3½ years

Daniel Reference:

While the term "1,260 days" is not explicit in Daniel, it fits within the midpoint-to-end structure of the 70th week (Daniel 9:27) and is implied in the persecution period of Daniel 7:25.

4. The 1,290 Days

"And from the time that the daily sacrifice is taken away… there shall be one thousand two hundred and ninety days."

Daniel 12:11 NKJV

This extends the timeline by 30 extra days beyond the 1,260-day tribulation. It suggests a period for:

- Cleansing the desecrated temple

- Final judgments on the beast system

- Preparation for Christ's millennial reign

Revelation Parallel:

While Revelation does not mention the 1,290 days specifically, the cleansing will occur after the seven bowls of the wrath of God and destruction of Babylonian nations at Armageddon Revelation 16–19 NKJV

5. The 1,335 Days

"Blessed is he who waits and comes to the one thousand three hundred and thirty-five days."
Daniel 12:12 NKJV

This extends 45 days beyond the 1,290—a total of 75 days after the tribulation ends.

- Likely refers to a time of restoration and preparation of the temple and the city of Jerusalem after the cleansing. This cleansing of the temple is supernatural because the Kings of kings and the Lord of lords can not dowel in a defiled temple.

Revelation Connection:

Though not directly mentioned, this aligns with Revelation 19–20—the Millennial Kingdom inauguration and rewards for the faithful.

6. The 2,300 Evenings and Mornings

"For two thousand three hundred days; then the sanctuary shall be cleansed." Daniel 8:14 NKJV

This prophecy originally pointed to the desecration under Antiochus Epiphanes, but may also look forward to:

The future desecration by the Antichrist

- Restoration and cleansing of the sanctuary at Christ's return

Revelation Application:

The desecration and ultimate cleansing of the temple (heavenly and/or earthly) is seen in:

- Revelation 11:1–2 (Gentiles trampling the holy city)

- Revelation 15–16 (judgment and purification before Christ returns)

Chart: Time Alignment Between Daniel and Revelation

Daniel's Time Prophecy	Length	Revelation Equivalent	Purpose/Context
70 Weeks (9:24–27)	490 years	Chapters 6–19	Timeline of Israel, Messiah, Tribulation
Final Week (9:27)	7 years	Tribulation	Antichrist covenant & betrayal
Half of Week	3½ years	42 months / 1,260 days	Great Tribulation
Time, Times, ½ Time	3½ years	42 months / 1,260 days	Persecution of saints
1,260 Days	3½ years	Rev. 11, 12, 13	Prophecy, protection, persecution
1,290 Days	+30 days	Implied in Rev. 16–19	Wrath, judgment, temple cleansing
1,335 Days	+45 days	Implied in Rev. 19–20	Blessing, resurrection, reward
2,300 Days	~6.3 years	Echoed in Rev. 11–16	Desecration and restoration

Conclusion: God's Calendar Is Precise

From Daniel to Revelation, we see a prophetic symmetry that proves the hand of God in both history and the future. These time periods were not merely for Daniel's understanding, but for ours—so that we would be prepared.

As these days draw near, the wise will understand.

"But the wise shall understand."
Daniel 12:10, NKJV

CHAPTER 12:
THE BEAST, THE FALSE PROPHET, AND THE SEVEN HEADS

"He shall even rise against the Prince of princes; but he shall be broken without human means."
Daniel 8:25, NKJV

From the earliest visions of Daniel to the terrifying imagery of Revelation, a sinister figure reappears across time and prophecy: the little horn, the man of sin, the beast, and the false prophet. These are not four different individuals but a composite picture of Satan's final counterfeit system—a religious-political alliance energized by the dragon himself.

In this chapter, we will bring together the prophetic strands from Daniel and Revelation to reveal the identity, rise, and ultimate fall of this last great enemy of God and His people.

1. The Little Horn in Daniel: A Seed of Rebellion

In Daniel 7, the prophet sees a vision of four great beasts rising from the sea. The fourth, more terrifying than the rest, has ten horns, and among them rises a little horn:

"There was another horn, a little one, coming up among them… and in this horn, were eyes like the eyes of a man, and a mouth speaking pompous words." (Daniel 7:8)

This little horn speaks blasphemy, persecutes the saints, and attempts to change times and laws (v. 25). He is allowed to rule for "a time and times and half a time"—3½ years, the same period mentioned in Revelation 13.

In Daniel 8, the little horn appears again—growing exceedingly great, exalting itself as high as the Prince of the host, removing the daily sacrifice, and casting truth to the ground. Though many view Antiochus Epiphanes as a partial fulfillment, the angel makes it clear:

"The vision refers to the time of the end."
Daniel 8:17 NKJV

The little horn is not merely a historical ruler—it is the spirit of Antichrist, culminating in a final global figure.

2. The Beast from the Sea in Revelation: The Little Horn Fully Revealed

In Revelation 13, this figure reappears as the beast rising out of the sea—but now in full form:

"And I saw a beast rising up out of the sea, having seven heads and ten horns, and on his horns ten crowns, and on his heads a blasphemous name."
Revelation 13:1 NKJV

He is empowered by the dragon (Satan), receives a deadly wound that is healed, and becomes the object of global worship:

"The dragon gave him his power, his throne, and great authority."

This beast makes war with the saints, rules for 42 months (3½ years), and controls commerce, requiring all to receive his mark to buy or sell.

3. The Connection Between the Dragon and the Beast

In Revelation 12, the dragon is described as:

"A great, fiery red dragon having seven heads and ten horns, and seven diadems on his heads."
Revelation 12:3 NKJV

This is Satan, and his features mirror those of the beast in Revelation 13.

Chapter	Entity	Description	Crowns On
Rev 12	Dragon	7 heads, 10 horns	Heads
Rev 13	Beast	7 heads, 10 horns	Horns

This shift is crucial:

- In Revelation 12, Satan rules through spiritual-religious empires, thus the crowns are on the heads.

- In Revelation 13, the beast rules through political power, so the crowns move to the ten horns—standing for modern nations under Antichrist's control.

The seven heads, now marked with blasphemous names, represent modern religious authorities, particularly the seven papal heads of the Roman Catholic Church, who have exalted themselves with divine titles and led the world into spiritual harlotry.

4. The Beast System: A Modern Rebirth of Ancient Evil

The seven heads with blasphemous names symbolize a system of false worship, deception, and idolatry. These are not ancient empires but modern religious powers, led by the papacy, claiming to be Christ while denying His truth.

> *"On his heads a blasphemous name."*
> *Rev. 13:1 NKJV*

This fulfills the description of Mystery Babylon—the mother of harlots:

> *"And on her forehead a name was written MYSTERY, BABYLON*
> *THE GREAT, THE MOTHER OF HARLOTS AND OF THE*
> *ABOMINATIONS OF THE EARTH."*
> *Revelation 17:5 NKJV*

The Roman Catholic Church is not just a denomination—it is a false religious empire, the continuation of Babylon's rebellion, merging paganism with Christianity and uniting political and spiritual power under the pope.

5. The Second Beast: The False Prophet

> *"Then I saw another beast coming up out of the earth, and he had two*
> *horns like a lamb and spoke like a dragon."*
> *Revelation 13:11 NKJV*

This second beast looks like a lamb—a false Christ or counterfeit Church—but speaks like a dragon, revealing his true origin.

He:

- Performs great signs

- Calls down fire from heaven (false Pentecost)

- Creates and animates an image of the beast

- Requires all to worship the image

- Enforces the mark of the beast

This is the False Prophet, the religious counterpart to the Antichrist, the papal system fulfills this role. The pope, revered as "Holy Father" and "Vicar of Christ," fits the prophetic pattern of blasphemous spiritual authority used to lead the world into deception.

Together, the beast from the sea (Antichrist) and the beast from the earth (False Prophet) form a satanic counterfeit trinity with the dragon (Satan):

- Dragon = False Father

- Beast = False Christ

- False Prophet = False Spirit

6. The Fall of the False Church

Though Mystery Babylon rides the beast for a time—using political power to expand her religious reach—she is eventually destroyed by the very kings she once controlled:

"The ten horns... will hate the harlot, make her desolate and naked, eat her flesh and burn her with fire."

Revelation 17:16 NJKV

The beast will abolish false religion to centralize worship around himself, declaring himself as god in the temple

"Who opposes and exalts himself above all that is called God or that is worshiped, so that he sits as God in the temple of God, showing himself that he is God."
II Thessalonians 2:4 NKJV

7. The Destruction of the Beast System

Though terrifying, the end of this system is certain and swift.

"And then the lawless one will be revealed, whom the Lord will consume

with the breath of His mouth and destroy with the brightness of His
coming."
II Thessalonians 2:8 NKJV

"Then the beast was captured, and with him the false prophet who
worked signs in his presence, by which he deceived those who received
the mark of the beast and those who worshiped his image. These two
were cast alive into the lake of fire burning with brimstone."
Revelation 19:20 NKJV

The little horn, the Antichrist, and the False Prophet—this unholy trinity—will be destroyed by Christ Himself at His return.

Conclusion: Truth Overcomes the Lie

The Word of God does not leave us in confusion. While the beast rises with modern religious and political power, while he deceives through the false prophet and is worshiped by the world—he will fall. The saints will reign. And the false system called Mystery Babylon will be no more.

"Then the kingdom and dominion, And the greatness of the kingdoms
under the whole heaven, shall be given to the people, the saints of the
Most High. His kingdom is an everlasting kingdom, and all dominions
shall serve and obey Him.'"
Daniel 7:27 NKJV

Chapter 13:
The Coming of the King of Kings and Lord of Lords

"Now I saw heaven opened, and behold, a white horse. And He who sat on him was called Faithful and True, and in righteousness He judges and makes war. His eyes were like a flame of fire, and on His head were many crowns. He had a name written that no one knew except Himself. He was clothed with a robe dipped in blood, and His name is called The Word of God. And the armies in heaven, clothed in fine linen, white and clean, followed Him on white horses. Now out of His mouth goes a sharp sword, that with it He should strike the nations. And He Himself will rule them with a rod of iron. He Himself treads the winepress of the fierceness and wrath of Almighty God. And He has on His robe and on His thigh a name written: KING OF KINGS AND LORD OF LORDS."
Revelation 19:11-16 NKJV

All of history is building toward one climactic moment—the return of the Lord Jesus Christ. Not as a suffering servant, but as a conquering King. Not in meekness, but in might. This is the blessed hope of the saints, the dreadful fear of the rebellious, and the final unveiling of the glory of the Son of God.

But what does the Bible really say about His coming? And what must take place before that glorious day?

1. The Word "Coming" – Greek Meaning and Prophetic Weight

The word often translated as "coming" in the New Testament is the Greek word parousia (παρουσία). This word does not merely refer to someone's arrival—it describes the royal presence of a king, often used in ancient times for the official state visit of a monarch or emperor. It implies authority, power, and splendor.

Jesus used this word repeatedly in Matthew 24:

- "What will be the sign of Your coming and of the end of the age?" (v. 3)

- "As the lightning comes from the east and flashes to the west, so also will the coming of the Son of Man be." (v. 27)

The parousia is not hidden or symbolic. It is visible, glorious, and world-shaking.

2. Signs on the Earth Before His Coming

Jesus, in the Olivet Discourse (Matthew 24; Mark 13; Luke 21), laid out straightforward signs that would take place on the earth before His return:

The Beginning of Sorrows (Matthew 24:6–8)

These are signs that affect nations and nature:

- Wars and rumors of wars

- Nations rising against nations

- Famines

- Pestilences (plagues, pandemics)

- Earthquakes in various places

Jesus said, "All these are the beginning of sorrows." These are birth pains—not the end, but the start of intensifying labor.

Persecution and Apostasy (Matthew 24:9–12)

- Believers will be hated and killed

- Many will be offended, betray one another, and hate one another

- False prophets will arise

- Lawlessness will abound

- The love of many will grow cold

The Global Witness

"And this gospel of the kingdom will be preached in all the world as a witness to all the nations, and then the end will come."

Matthew 24:14 NKJV

Before the end, the true gospel will go to all peoples—not just church tradition, but the truth of Christ crucified, risen, and coming again.

3. Signs in the Heavens

As the end draws near, the heavens themselves will testify to the nearness of the King:

""Immediately after the tribulation of those days the sun will be

darkened, and the moon will not give its light; the stars will fall from heaven, and the powers of the heavens will be shaken."
Matthew 24:29 NKJV

These cosmic signs are echoed in Revelation 6:

- Sun becomes black as sackcloth

- Moon becomes like blood

- Stars fall to the earth

- Sky recedes like a scroll

- Every mountain and island are moved

These are not poetic metaphors—Scripture presents them as literal, terrifying disruptions of the created order, announcing the coming wrath of the Lamb.

4. Revelation: The Seals, Trumpets, and Bowls – A Sequential Pattern of Judgment

In the book of Revelation, we find a divine sequence of judgments that unfold leading up to Christ's return. These events run parallel to and intensify the signs Jesus gave in the Gospels.

The Seven Seals (Revelation 6–8) – The Beginning of Tribulation

1. White Horse – Conquest (false peace, deception of Antichrist)

2. Red Horse – War and bloodshed

3. Black Horse – Famine and economic collapse

4. Pale Horse – Death by sword, hunger, beasts

5. Martyrs Cry Out – Persecution of the faithful

6. Cosmic Disturbances – Earthquake, darkened sun, blood moon, stars fall

7. Silence in Heaven – Prelude to the next wave of judgment

These match the beginning of sorrows and great tribulation Jesus' spoke of.

The Seven Trumpets (Revelation 8–11) – Judgments Intensify

1. Hail and fire destroy vegetation

2. Burning mountain falls into the sea (one-third of sea turns to blood)

3. Wormwood star poisons waters

4. Sun, moon, and stars darkened

5. Locusts from the Abyss torment for five months

6. Four angels released – massive war and death

7. Kingdom declared – final woe is coming

These judgments affect both creation and humanity. The warnings grow more severe, yet people still do not repent.

The Seven Bowls of Wrath (Revelation 16) – Final and Total

1. Painful sores on those with the mark

2. Sea becomes blood

3. Rivers become blood

4. Sun scorches men with fire

5. Darkness and pain in the beast's kingdom

6. Euphrates dries up to prepare the way for kings of the East

7.   Massive earthquake, hailstones, and Babylon judged

By the time the bowls are poured out, the world is ripe for judgment. The system of the beast is fully set up—and about to be destroyed by the coming of the King.

5. The Sign of the Son of Man and the Return in Glory

"Then the sign of the Son of Man will appear in heaven, and then all the tribes of the earth will mourn... and they will see the Son of Man coming on the clouds of heaven with power and great glory." (Matthew 24:30)

- The sky will split open

- Every eye will see Him (Revelation 1:7)

- The heavens will be filled with the armies of heaven

- He will descend riding a white horse, clothed in a robe dipped in blood

6. The King of Kings Returns (Revelation 19:11–16)

"Now I saw heaven opened…"

- Faithful and True – His name and His nature

- Eyes like flame of fire – all-seeing judgment

- Many crowns – ultimate and total authority

- The Word of God – riding in righteousness

- The armies of heaven follow Him

- Out of His mouth a sharp sword – slays the nations

- KING OF KINGS AND LORD OF LORDS – written on His robe and thigh

This is no secret rapture—it is the glorious, visible, unstoppable return of Christ to judge, conquer, and reign.

7. What Happens at His Coming

- The beast and false prophet are captured and cast into the lake of fire (Revelation 19:20)

- The armies of the earth are slain by the sword from His mouth

- Satan is bound for 1,000 years (Revelation 20:1–3)

- The saints reign with Christ (Revelation 20:4–6)

Are You Ready for the King?

The signs are not random—they are warnings and invitations. The parousia of the Lord Jesus is not just a return; it is the consummation of all prophecy, the end of all rebellion, and the beginning of His righteous reign.

"He who testifies to these things says, 'Surely I am coming quickly.'
Amen. Even so, come, Lord Jesus!"
Revelation 22:20 NKJV

The Snatching of the Church — Before, Mid, or After the Tribulation?

"Then we who are alive and remain shall be caught up together with
them in the clouds to meet the Lord in the air. And thus, we shall always
be with the Lord."
1 Thessalonians 4:17, NKJV NKJV

Few subjects have stirred more debate within Christian theology than the question of when the Church will be taken up—snatched away from the earth to meet the Lord in the air. This event is commonly called the rapture, a term not found in Scripture itself, but popularized through centuries of tradition and interpretation, especially by Roman Catholic theologians.

To rightly divide this truth, we must first go back to the original language of the Bible and clarify what the Word of God says.

1. The Greek Word: Harpazō – Snatching by Force

The word "rapture" comes from the Latin Vulgate translation of 1 Thessalonians 4:17, where the phrase "caught up" was translated as rapiemur from rapturo, meaning "to seize or snatch."

But the original Greek word used by the apostle Paul is:

Harpazō (ἁρπάζω) – "to seize by force, to snatch away suddenly"

This word appears in several places:

- Acts 8:39 – Philip is "caught away" by the Spirit of the Lord

- 2 Corinthians 12:2 – Paul is "caught up" to the third heaven

- Revelation 12:5 – The male child (Christ) is "caught up" to God and His throne

It is a forceful, supernatural removal. In the context of 1 Thessalonians 4:16–17, it refers to a dramatic event where believers, both dead and living, are united with Christ in the clouds.

2. The Foundational Text: 1 Thessalonians 4:13–18

Paul, under divine inspiration, writes to comfort believers who were mourning the dead:

"But I do not want you to be ignorant, brethren, concerning those who have fallen asleep, lest you sorrow as others who have no hope. For if we believe that Jesus died and rose again, even so God will bring with Him those who sleep in Jesus. For this we say to you by the word of the Lord, that we who are alive and remain until the coming of the Lord will by no means precede those who are asleep. For the Lord Himself will descend from heaven with a shout, with the voice of an archangel, and

*with the trumpet of God. And the dead in Christ will rise first. Then we
who are alive and remain shall be caught up together with them in the
clouds to meet the Lord in the air. And thus, we shall always be with the
Lord. Therefore comfort one another with these words."*
I Thessalonians 4:13-18 NKJV

*"For the Lord Himself will descend from heaven with a shout… And the
dead in Christ will rise first. Then we who are alive and remain shall be
caught up [harpazō]… and thus we shall always be with the Lord."*

This is a real, physical event. The snatching occurs after the
resurrection of those who have died in Christ. It is not secret or symbolic—
it is described as:

- With a shout

- With the voice of an archangel

- With the trumpet of God

These details are significant because they mirror other prophecies in
Scripture, especially those in Matthew 24 and 1 Corinthians 15.

3. Three Major Views on the Timing of the Snatching

This is where most division arises. Let us explore each position with
its strengths and scriptural references:

Pre-Tribulation View

- Belief: The Church is snatched before the 7-year tribulation
  begins.

- Key arguments:

  - God has not appointed us to wrath

*"For God did not appoint us to wrath, but to obtain salvation through
our Lord Jesus Christ,"*

- The Church is absent from Revelation chapters 6–18

- The snatching is "imminent," with no signs preceding it

The most miss understood scripture for those who hold to this view is revelation 3:10

"Because you have kept My command to persevere, I also will keep you from the hour of trial which shall come upon the whole world, to test those who dwell on the earth."
Revelation 3:10 NKJV

Clearly the scripture says that there is the hour of trail (test) which shall come upon the entire world no exceptions to test those who dwell on the earth believers in Christ and unbelievers alike no exceptions. Then the scripture says but those Christians and I use the word Christians loosely because not all Christians will make it to the end but will apostasy from the faith due to deception and pressure of life. But true believers, those who live by faith and not by sight and keep the command to persevere, the Lord will keep them from the hour of testing that is coming on the earth. The key word here is the word keep, this word keep in the Greek text means to guard and not to snatch. The Lord will give divine protection and provision to the believers to persevere through the hour of testing.

"No temptation has overtaken you except such as is common to man; but God is faithful, who will not allow you to be tempted beyond what you are able, but with the temptation will also make the way of escape, that you may be able to bear it."
I Corinthians 10:13 NKJV

Mid-Tribulation View

- Belief: The Church is snatched in the middle of the 7 years, after the abomination of desolation and before the great wrath.

- Key arguments:

    - The two witnesses are raised and taken up around the midpoint

"And they heard a loud voice from heaven saying to them, "Come up here." And they ascended to heaven in a cloud, and their enemies saw them."
Revelation 11:12 NKJV

    - The 7th trumpet (Rev 11:15) may correspond to the "last trumpet" in (1 Corinthians 15:52)

"Then the seventh angel sounded: And there were loud voices in heaven, saying, "The kingdoms of this world have become the kingdoms of our Lord and of His Christ, and He shall reign forever and ever!""
Revelation 11:15 NKJV

"In a moment, in the twinkling of an eye, at the last trumpet. For the trumpet will sound, and the dead will be raised incorruptible, and we shall be changed."
I Corinthians 15:52 NKJV

    - The Church is preserved but present during the first half

Post-Tribulation View

- Belief: The Church goes through the full tribulation and is snatched at the visible return of Christ.

- Key arguments:

    - Jesus said, "Immediately after the tribulation… He will send His angels… and gather His elect"

""Immediately after the tribulation of those days the sun will be darkened, and the moon will not give its light; the stars will fall from heaven, and the powers of the heavens will be shaken. Then the sign of

the Son of Man will appear in heaven, and then all the tribes of the earth will mourn, and they will see the Son of Man coming on the clouds of heaven with power and great glory. And He will send His angels with a great sound of a trumpet, and they will gather together His elect from the four winds, from one end of heaven to the other."
Matthew 24:29-31 NKJV

Revelation 20:4–6 says the saints are raised after the beast is judged

"And I saw thrones, and they sat on them, and judgment was committed to them. Then I saw the souls of those who had been beheaded for their witness to Jesus and for the word of God, who had not worshiped the beast or his image, and had not received his mark on their foreheads or on their hands. And they lived and reigned with Christ for a thousand years. But the rest of the dead did not live again until the thousand years were finished. This is the first resurrection. Blessed and holy is he who has part in the first resurrection. Over such the second death has no power, but they shall be priests of God and of Christ and shall reign with Him a thousand years.
Revelation 20:4-6 NKJV

This Saints are not that of the snatched church who are going to come back with the Lord but these saints are those who will be killed during the last three and half years tribulations.

Emphasizes endurance and overcoming

"He who leads into captivity shall go into captivity; he who kills with the sword must be killed with the sword. Here is the patience and the faith of the saints."
Revelation 13:10 NKJV

4. Contrasting the Key Texts

Scripture	Theme	Implication
1 Thess. 4:16–17	Resurrection and snatching	Loud, visible event with a trumpet

Scripture	Theme	Implication
1 Cor. 15:51–52	Instant transformation at the last trumpet	Suggests timing at the end of trumpet judgment
Matt. 24:29–31	Elect gathered after tribulation	Linked to the visible return of Christ
Rev. 11:15	The seventh trumpet sounds	Kingdom declared, could parallel 1 Cor. 15
Rev. 14:14–16	A "harvest" by the Son of Man with a sickle	Could symbolize the snatching at the final stage

5. A Call for Truth and Readiness

The debate is not merely theological—it affects how we live, watch, and prepare. Regardless of the timing, Scripture calls us to:

. Be ready:

"Therefore, you also be ready, for the Son of Man is com "Therefore you also be ready, for the Son of Man is coming at an hour you do not expect."

. Watch and be sober:

"Therefore, let us not sleep, as others do, but let us watch and be sober."

. Endure to the end:

"But he who endures to the end shall be saved."
Matthew 24:13 NKJV

. Keep our lamps full and hearts pure:

""Then the kingdom of heaven shall be likened to ten virgins who took their lamps and went out to meet the bridegroom. Now five of them were wise, and five were foolish. Those who were foolish took their lamps and took no oil with them, but while the bridegroom was delayed, they all slumbered and slept. "And at midnight a cry was heard: 'Behold, the bridegroom is coming; go out to meet him!' Then all those virgins

arose and trimmed their lamps. And the foolish said to the wise, 'Give us some of your oil, for our lamps are going out.' But the wise answered, saying, 'No, lest there should not be enough for us and you; but go rather to those who sell, and buy for yourselves.' And while they went to buy, the bridegroom came, and those who were ready went in with him to the wedding; and the door was shut. "Afterward the other virgins came also, saying, 'Lord, Lord, open to us!' But he answered and said, 'Assuredly, I say to you, I do not know you.' "Watch therefore, for you know neither the day nor the hour in which the Son of Man is coming."
Matthew 25:1-3, 5-13 NKJV

We must not divide over timing but be united in faith, holiness, and urgency. Whether the Lord comes today, midway, or at the end—let Him find us faithful.

Conclusion: A Word of Caution and Hope

While tradition may call it "rapture," the Word calls it a snatching—and it is real. Let no one deceive you with man-made dates or fearful theories. The Son of Man is coming at an hour no one expects.

"Therefore comfort one another with these words."
1 Thessalonians 4:18 NKJV

CHAPTER 14: INDULGE ME FOR A MOMENT

My understanding on some matters.

"Be diligent to present yourself approved to God, a worker who does not need to be ashamed, rightly dividing the word of truth."

How do we find ourselves approved to God? By being diligent that is to be prompt by substantiating the word of God by handling it correctly in a straight path. The miss understanding comes from the word wrath of God, yes to rightly divide the word of truth we who will be found blameless at the coming of the Lord are not appointed to the wrath of God. What we fell to understand is that the are two wraths in the book of revelation.

"And said to the mountains and rocks, "Fall on us and hide us from the face of Him who sits on the throne and from the wrath of the Lamb! For the great day of His wrath has come, and who is able to stand?""
Revelation 6:16-17 NKJV

From the wrath of the Lamb! There is no were in the Bible where God is called the Lamb. This title only applies to the Lord Jesus Christ who is the Lamb of God. Revelation 6 deals with the unveiling of the seven seals and after the unsealing of the seals comes the seven trumpets, these seven trumpets are the wrath of the Lord Jesus Christ and after the seven trumpets comes the seven bowls which are the wrath of God

"Then I heard a loud voice from the temple saying to the seven angels,
"Go and pour out the bowls of the wrath of God on the earth.""
Revelation 16:1 NKJV

These seven wraths of God are the ones we believers in Christ are not appointed to. And these seven wraths of God occur just after the Antichrist set up the abomination of desolation in the temple.

"For God did not appoint us to wrath, but to obtain salvation through
our Lord Jesus Christ,"
I Thessalonians 5:9 NKJV

This is my understanding on this matter, those believers who will be found blameless and Holy at the coming of the Lord will be snatched before the wrath of God which puts this event to occur mid tribulations. This is just my assumption. But i still hold to the belief that what ever our views are, we are to live honorable and blameless.

"So that He may establish your hearts blameless in holiness before our
God and Father at the coming of our Lord Jesus Christ with all His
saints."
I Thessalonians 3:13 NKJV

"in the body of His flesh through death, to present you holy, and
blameless, and above reproach in His sight— if indeed you continue
in the faith, grounded and steadfast, and are not moved away from
the hope of the gospel which you heard, which was preached to every
creature under heaven, of which I, Paul, became a minister."
Colossians 1:22-23 NKJV

One last matter i would like to address is found in the letter to the Thessalonians.

"Now, brethren, concerning the coming of our Lord Jesus Christ and our gathering together to Him, we ask you, not to be soon shaken in mind or troubled, either by spirit or by word or by letter, as if from us, as though the day of Christ had come. Let no one deceive you by any means; for that Day will not come unless the falling away comes first, and the man of sin is revealed, the son of perdition," "who opposes and exalts himself above all that is called God or that is worshiped, so that he sits as God in the temple of God, showing himself that he is God."
II Thessalonians 2:1-4 NKJV

To rightly divide the word of truth, the day of the coming of the Lord will not come unless the falling away comes first, the apostasy from the faith in Christ. Believers will turn away from the truth.

"For the time will come when they will not endure sound doctrine, but according to their own desires, because they have itching ears, they will heap up for themselves teachers; and they will turn their ears away from the truth and be turned aside to fables."
II Timothy 4:3-4 NKJV

This sign will come first which we are already in it and then the man of sin, one of the names of the Antichrist is revealed, the son of perdition. The apostasy comes first then the Antichrist will be revealed, this is all before the coming day of the Lord. By this we now know that the Antichrist will be ruling before the church is snatched away.

V4 tells us what the Antichrist will do at the middle of the seven years. This is what will bring forth the wrath of God, the abomination of desolation. This is when the snatching will take place right before the wrath of God.

"Then I looked, and behold, a white cloud, and on the cloud sat One like the Son of Man, having on His head a golden crown, and in His hand a

sharp sickle. And another angel came out of the temple, crying with a loud voice to Him who sat on the cloud, "Thrust in Your sickle and reap, for the time has come for You to reap, for the harvest of the earth is ripe." So, He who sat on the cloud thrust in His sickle on the earth, and the earth was reaped."
Revelation 14:14-16 NKJV

Then the apostle Paul goes on to tell us what is restraining the Antichrist from being revealed at this moment in time.

"Do you not remember that when I was still with you, I told you these things? And now you know what is restraining, that he may be revealed in his own time. For the mystery of lawlessness is already at work; only he who now restrains will do so until he is taken out of the way. And then the lawless one will be revealed, whom the Lord will consume with the breath of His mouth and destroy with the brightness of His coming. The coming of the lawless one is according to the working of Satan, with all power, signs, and lying wonders,"
II Thessalonians 2:5-9 NKJV

Now this is where things get interesting. The apostle Paul tells us what is now restraining the Antichrist from being revealed, the mystery of lawlessness which is already at work. It doses not say anything about the church or the Holy Spirit but about the lawlessness and who is the father of lawlessness? The devil. So, the devil is the one restraining the Antichrist from being revealed. The word restraining in the Greek means to hold down or back.

So only he the devil who now restrains will do so until he the devil is taken out of the way, and how will he be taken out of the way and from where? Well, this why I love the word of God. It does not leave us wanting but always confirms itself. This word taken in Greek implies an intensive event coming into being, to arise or appear.

"And war broke out in heaven: Michael and his angels fought with the dragon; and the dragon and his angels fought, but they did not

prevail, nor was a place found for them in heaven any longer. So, the great dragon was cast out, that serpent of old, called the Devil and Satan, who deceives the whole world; he was cast to the earth, and his angels were cast out with him. Then I heard a loud voice saying in heaven, "Now salvation, and strength, and the kingdom of our God, and the power of His Christ have come, for the accuser of our brethren, who accused them before our God day and night, has been cast down. And they overcame him by the blood of the Lamb and by the word of their testimony, and they did not love their lives to the death. Therefore rejoice, O heavens, and you who dwell in them! Woe to the inhabitants of the earth and the sea! For the devil has come down to you, having great wrath, because he knows that he has a short time.""
Revelation 12:7-12 NKJV

Only when this happens will the Antichrist be revealed and unfortunately the church will be still on the earth

"And the dragon was enraged with the woman, and he went to make war with the rest of her offspring, who keep the commandments of God and have the testimony of Jesus Christ."
Revelation 12:17 NKJV

The woman here is Israel and those who keep the commandments of God and have the testimony of Jesus Christ are Christians the church. Right after revelation 12 the beast is seen rising out of the sea in chapter 13, the beast is the Antichrist, and the devil will give him power and authority to rule the world for seven years.

In conclusion: there are still some events that must happen before the coming of the Lord. The word of God is forever settled in heaven, so God can not go against His own word or else He will be found a lier, and we know that God is not a man that He should lie nor a son of man that He should repent.

Chapter 15:
The Snatching of the Church — Supper, War, and the Kingdom

"Let us be glad and rejoice and give Him glory, for the marriage of the Lamb has come, and His wife has made herself ready."
Revelation 19:7, NKJV NKJV

History is not spiraling into chaos—it is marching toward a coronation. The return of Jesus Christ is not only about judgment but about union, celebration, victory, and rule. This chapter unveils the culmination of God's prophetic timeline: the reunion of the Bride with the Bridegroom, the defeat of evil, and the establishment of the righteous reign of the King of kings.

1. The Meeting in the Air: The Bridegroom Welcomes His Bride

"Then we who are alive and remain shall be caught up together with

them in the clouds to meet the Lord in the air."
1 Thessalonians 4:17 NKJV

The Greek word for "meet" in this passage is apantēsis (ἀπάντησις), which refers to a formal reception of a dignitary. In ancient times, when a king approached a city, the citizens would go out to meet him in honor and escort him back in triumph.

This is exactly what happens when the saints are caught up to meet Christ. It is not a fleeing—it is a royal procession. We meet the Lord in the air, transformed in the twinkling of an eye, adorned for the Bridegroom.

"And thus, we shall always be with the Lord."
1 Thess. 4:17 NKJV

2. The Marriage Supper of the Lamb: The Great Celebration

"Then he said to me, "Write: 'Blessed are those who are called to the marriage supper of the Lamb!'" And he said to me, "These are the true sayings of God.""

The next scene in heaven is one of feasting and joy. The long-awaited union between Christ and His Church is now publicly declared in glory. This is not symbolic—it is real, prophetic fulfillment.

The bride:

- Made ready

- Clothed in fine linen, bright and clean

- Are the righteous acts of the saints (Rev. 19:8)

This supper is not just a heavenly event—it signals that the bride will now rule and reign with her King.

3. The Return with the Armies of Heaven: The King on

the White Horse

"Now I saw heaven opened, and behold, a white horse. And He who sat on him was called Faithful and True, and in righteousness He judges and makes war. His eyes were like a flame of fire, and on His head were many crowns. He had a name written that no one knew except Himself. And the armies in heaven, clothed in fine linen, white and clean, followed Him on white horses."

From celebration to confrontation—the Lord does not delay. Heaven opens and the King rides forth:

- His name is Faithful and True

- He judges in righteousness

- His eyes are like flames of fire

- On His head are many crowns

- He wears a robe dipped in blood

- His name is The Word of God

- He is followed by the armies of heaven, clothed in fine linen (the saints!)

He does not return alone. The redeemed ride with Him—not to fight, but to witness the Word of His mouth defeat the enemies of God.

4. The Battle of Armageddon: The Beast's Army Destroyed

"And I saw the beast, the kings of the earth, and their armies, gathered together to make war against Him who sat on the horse and against His army."

The kings of the earth and their armies are gathered at Armageddon (Rev. 16:16). The beast and the false prophet deceive them. But their rebellion is met with divine fury.

"Out of His mouth goes a sharp sword, that with it He should strike the
nations."
Rev. 19:15 NKJV

There is no struggle—the King speaks, and the enemy is defeated.

"For wherever the carcass is, there the eagles will be gathered
together."
Matthew 24:28 NKJV

""And as for you, son of man, thus says the Lord God, 'Speak to every
sort of bird and to every beast of the field: "Assemble yourselves and
come; Gather together from all sides to My sacrificial meal Which I
am sacrificing for you, A great sacrificial meal on the mountains of
Israel, That you may eat flesh and drink blood. You shall eat the flesh
of the mighty, Drink the blood of the princes of the earth, Of rams and
lambs, Of goats and bulls, All of them fatlings of Bashan. You shall eat
fat till you are full, and drink blood till you are drunk, At My sacrificial
meal Which I am sacrificing for you. You shall be filled at My table with
horses and riders, with mighty men and with all the men of war," says
the Lord God."
Ezekiel 39:17-20 NKJV

"And all the birds were filled with their flesh."
Rev. 19:21NKJV

As i author this book this event is in the making as wars and rumors
of wars are echoing between Israel and Iran.

This gruesome scene contrasts the wedding feast of the Lamb with
the carrion feast of judgment. One supper is for the righteous—this one,
for the rebellious.

5. The Judgment of the Beast and the False Prophet

"Then the beast was captured, and with him the false prophet who worked signs in his presence, by which he deceived those who received the mark of the beast and those who worshiped his image. These two were cast alive into the lake of fire burning with brimstone."
Revelation 19:20 NKJV

This is the first instance of eternal judgment being executed.

- The beast (Antichrist)

- The false prophet (religious deceiver)

They are not merely defeated—they are cast alive into the lake of fire, bypassing any earthly death. Their judgment is final, eternal, and unchangeable.

6. The Binding of Satan for 1,000 Years

"He laid hold of the dragon, that serpent of old, who is the Devil and Satan, and bound him for a thousand years;"
Revelation 20:2 NKJV

The dragon, also called the serpent of old, the Devil, and Satan, is bound and cast into the bottomless pit (Abyss). For a full millennium:

- He cannot deceive the nations

- He cannot influence governments or religions

- He is shut up and sealed

The adversary of God and man is now silenced.

7. The Kingdom of Christ is Established

"And I saw thrones, and they sat on them, and judgment was committed to them. Then I saw the souls of those who had for their witness to Jesus and for the word of God, who had not worshiped the beast or his image, and had not received his mark on their foreheads or on their

hands. And they lived and reigned with Christ for a thousand years."
Revelation 20:4 NKJV

The saints—those beheaded for their testimony, those who overcame the beast—are raised to life and reign with Christ during this Millennial Kingdom.

This is:

- The answer to the disciples' question: "Will You at this time restore the kingdom to Israel?" (Acts 1:6)

- The fulfillment of Isaiah's prophecy: "Of the increase of His government and peace there will be no end…" (Isaiah 9:7)

Peace, righteousness, and justice now cover the earth as the King rules from Jerusalem.

Conclusion: The King Has Come

The journey is not over—but the Kingdom has come. The bride is with her Bridegroom, the enemy is defeated, and the true reign of Christ has begun.

Let the reader take hope. Let the Church be made ready. For the day draws near when the heavens will open again—and the One called Faithful and True will return.

"Blessed and holy is he who has part in the first resurrection. Over such the second death has no power, but they shall be priests of God and of Christ and shall reign with Him a thousand years."
Revelation 20:6 NKJV

Chapter 16:
Thrones, Resurrection, and the Reign of the Saints

"And I saw thrones, and they sat on them, and judgment was committed to them. Then I saw the souls of those who had been beheaded for their witness to Jesus and for the word of God, who had not worshiped the beast or his image, and had not received his mark on their foreheads or on their hands. And they lived and reigned with Christ for a thousand years."
Revelation 20:4 NKJV

The return of Jesus Christ does not merely bring judgment—it ushers in a new world order under the reign of righteousness. After the snatching of the Church, the Marriage Supper of the Lamb, the destruction of the beast and the false prophet, and the victorious return of the King of kings, one final adversary is still: the ancient serpent, the devil himself.

What follows next is a time unlike any the world has known a thousand years of divine rule and true peace on earth. This chapter captures the heart of that transition.

1. The Capture of Satan – Bound for a Thousand Years

"Then I saw an angel coming down from heaven, having the key to the bottomless pit and a great chain in his hand."
Revelation 20:1 NKJV

With divine authority, an angel seizes Satan—the deceiver of the entire world. He is:

- Bound with a chain

- Cast into the Abyss (bottomless pit)

- Sealed so he may deceive the nations no more

This is not symbolic. Satan's literal removal from the earthly realm signals the end of deception, warfare, and false religion. The beast and the false prophet are already in the lake of fire. Now Satan is restrained—his power is crushed for a specific and prophetic duration: one thousand years.

2. The Thrones Set Upon the Earth

"And I saw thrones, and they sat on them, and judgment was committed to them."
(Revelation 20:4) NKJV

Now we see a great reversal. The saints who were once despised and persecuted are now enthroned. These are not heavenly visions only—this is on earth, as the Millennial Kingdom begins.

Those given authority to sit on these thrones include:

- The twelve apostles (Matthew 19:28)

- Faithful overcomers from the churches (Revelation 2–3)

- The saints who refused the mark of the beast

- Those who endured to the end for Christ

This fulfills the promise made to the overcomers:

*"To him who overcomes I will grant to sit with Me on My throne, as I
also overcame and sat down with My Father on His throne."*
Revelation 3:21 NKJV

3. The First Resurrection – Martyrs Raised to Reign

*"And I saw thrones, and they sat on them, and judgment was committed
to them. Then I saw the souls of those who had been beheaded for their
witness to Jesus and for the word of God, who had not worshiped the
beast or his image, and had not received his mark on their foreheads or
on their hands. And they lived and reigned with Christ for a thousand
years."*
Revelation 20:4 NKJV

This is the first resurrection on earth after the return of the Lord.
These are:

- Not all the saved from every age

- Specifically, those who died during the tribulation

- Refused to worship the beast or his image

- Did not take his mark on their foreheads or hands

They are raised—bodily—and given the honor of reigning with Christ
during the Millennium.

*"But the rest of the dead did not live again until the thousand years were
finished. This is the first resurrection. Blessed and holy is he who has
part in the first resurrection. Over such the second death has no power,
but they shall be priests of God and of Christ and shall reign with Him a*

thousand years."
Revelation 20:5-6 NKJV

4. The Nature of the Millennial Kingdom

The thousand-year reign of Christ will be a time of:

- Perfect justice – Jesus will rule with a rod of iron (Revelation 2:27)

- Peace among nations – They will beat their swords into plowshares (Isaiah 2:4)

- Righteous government – Thrones set up in righteousness (Isaiah 32:1)

- Restored creation – The wolf shall dwell with the lamb (Isaiah 11:6)

"Behold, a king will reign in righteousness, and princes will rule with justice."
Isaiah 32:1 NKJV

"But with righteousness He shall judge the poor and decide with equity for the meek of the earth; He shall strike the earth with the rod of His mouth, and with the breath of His lips He shall slay the wicked. Righteousness shall be the belt of His loins, And faithfulness the belt of His waist. "The wolf also shall dwell with the lamb, The leopard shall lie down with the young goat, The calf and the young lion and the fatling together; And a little child shall lead them. The cow and the bear shall graze; Their young ones shall lie down together; And the lion shall eat straw like the ox. The nursing child shall play by the cobra's hole, And the weaned child shall put his hand in the viper's den. They shall not hurt nor destroy in all My holy mountain, For the earth shall be full of the knowledge of the Lord As the waters cover the sea."
Isaiah 11:4-9 NKJV

When the Prince of peace reign, there is peace indeed.

Jerusalem becomes the seat of government, and the saints serve as kingdom priests and rulers, fulfilling both spiritual and judicial functions.

"And has made us kings and priests to His God and Father, to Him be glory and dominion forever and ever. Amen."
Revelation 1:6 NKJV

5. A Kingdom With an End – For Now

This is not yet eternity. The thousand-year reign will end. Satan will be released for a final test of the nations (Revelation 20:7–10). But until then, the earth will see what it was always meant to be: a world under the rule of its true King, with redeemed humanity ruling beside Him.

Conclusion: The Fulfillment of All Things

With the devil bound, the saints enthroned, and the martyrs raised, the Millennial Kingdom begins. This is not allegory—it is the first phase of God's final redemptive plan. The curse is not yet removed, but righteousness rules. Death is not yet destroyed, but it is restrained. The kingdom is set up, and the King is reigning.

This is our hope. Not escape, but reign. Not fear, but faithfulness. Not fantasy, but fulfillment.

"And they shall reign with Him a thousand years."
(Revelation 20:6b) NKJV

Prophetic Timeline: From the Snatching to the Millennial Reign

1. The Snatching of the Church (1 Thessalonians 4:17; 1 Corinthians 15:52)
   - The saints, both dead and alive in Christ, are caught up to meet the Lord in the air.

- This marks the reunion of the Bride with the Bridegroom.

2. The Marriage Supper of the Lamb (Revelation 19:7–9)
   - The Church is presented in white linen.
   - A heavenly celebration of covenant and reward takes place before judgment falls.

3. The Return of Christ with the Armies of Heaven (Revelation 19:11–16)
   - Jesus descends visibly and gloriously on a white horse.
   - The armies of heaven, including the redeemed, follow Him.

4. The Battle of Armageddon (Revelation 19:17–21)
   - The beast, the false prophet, and the kings of the earth make war against Christ.
   - Jesus destroys them with the sword from His mouth.

5. Judgment of the Beast and the False Prophet (Revelation 19:20)
   - They are captured and cast alive into the lake of fire.
   - This is the first eternal judgment recorded in Scripture.

6. Binding of Satan for 1,000 Years (Revelation 20:1–3)
   - An angel binds the devil with a great chain.
   - He is sealed in the Abyss to prevent him from deceiving the nations.

7. The First Resurrection (Revelation 20:4–6)
   - Those beheaded for Christ during the tribulation are raised to reign.
   - They rule with Christ for a thousand years—the first resurrection.

8. The Millennial Reign of Christ (Revelation 20:4–6)
   - Thrones are set up on the earth.
   - The saints judge and rule with Christ in a world of peace and justice.

CHAPTER 17: ALL THINGS MADE NEW — GOD DWELLS WITH HIS PEOPLE

"Now when the thousand years have expired, Satan will be released
from his prison..."
Revelation 20:7, NKJV

The thousand years of peace ended—not because evil triumphs again, but because God's justice must be complete. Even after a millennium under Christ's perfect rule, the human heart—if untransformed—still chooses rebellion.

1. The Final Rebellion and the End of Satan

"And will go out to deceive the nations which are in the four corners
of the earth, Gog and Magog, to gather them together to battle, whose
number is as the sand of the sea."
Revelation 20:8 NKJV

From every corner of the earth, Gog and Magog gather in number like the sand of the sea. This is not a new army—it is the last gasp of defiance, the final exposing of every heart that still resists the rule of Christ.

But there is no war, no drawn-out battle.

"They went up on the breadth of the earth and surrounded the camp of the saints and the beloved city. And fire came down from God out of heaven and devoured them. The devil, who deceived them, was cast into the lake of fire and brimstone where the beast and the false prophet are. And they will be tormented day and night forever and ever."
Revelation 20:9-10 NKJV

Satan—the ancient dragon, the liar, the murderer, the accuser—is forever silenced. Not bound. Not banished. Judged.

2. The Great White Throne and the Judgment of All

"Then I saw a great white throne and Him who sat on it, from whose face the earth and the heaven fled away. And there was found no place for them."
Revelation 20:11 NKJV

Heaven and earth flee from His face—there is no hiding. Every soul that rejected the Lamb, every sinner not found in the Book of Life, stands before the King.

"And I saw the dead, small and great, standing before God, and books were opened. And another book was opened, which is the Book of Life. And the dead were judged according to their works, by the things which were written in the books. The sea gave up the dead who were in it, and Death and Hades delivered up the dead who were in them. And they were judged, each one according to his works. Then Death and Hades were cast into the lake of fire. This is the second death. And anyone not found written in the Book of Life was cast into the lake of fire."
Revelation 20:12-15 NKJV

This is not about cruelty—it is about justice. No injustice will remain. No evil will go unanswered. Every tear ever cried, every wrong ever endured, is answered.

Death and Hades are cast away. The second death comes—and then, eternity begins.

3. The New Heavens and the New Earth

"Now I saw a new heaven and a new earth, for the first heaven and the first earth had passed away. Also, there was no more sea."
Revelation 21:1 NKJV

Everything broken, fallen, and cursed is gone. This is not renovation. It is rebirth. The sea is no more. The pain, the division, the flood of grief— it is all behind.

And from heaven comes the jewel of all eternity:

4. The Holy City – New Jerusalem, the Bride of the Lamb

"Then I, John, saw the holy city, New Jerusalem, coming down out of heaven from God, prepared as a bride adorned for her husband."
Revelation 21:2 NKJV

The Bride of the King of Kings and the Lord of Lords on earth the Holy city, new Jerusalem and not the church for it was His bride in air after snatching. The church was glorified in Him in the heavens and now new Jerusalem will be glorified in Him on the earth and God can only dwell where His glory is perfected.

"And I heard a loud voice from heaven saying, "Behold, the tabernacle of God is with men, and He will dwell with them, and they shall be His people. God Himself will be with them and be their God. And God will wipe away every tear from their eyes; there shall be no more death, nor sorrow, nor crying. There shall be no more pain, for the former things

have passed away.""
Revelation 21:3-4 NKJV

He wipes away every tear. There is no more death, sorrow, crying, or pain. These former things are forever gone.

"Then He who sat on the throne said, "Behold, I make all things new."
And He said to me, "Write, for these words are true and faithful.""
Revelation 21:5 NKJV

5. God Dwells with His Own—Forever

At the beginning, God walked with Adam in the garden. He created man not for religion but for relationship—to dwell together in purity, joy, and unity. Sin shattered it. Babel rebelled. Babylon rose. Beasts reigned. But now—now it is finished.

- There is no temple—God and the Lamb are its temple.

- There is no sun or moon—the Lamb is its light.

- The gates are never shut—there is no night.

- The nations walk in the light of God's glory.

"And He said to me, "It is done! I am the Alpha and the Omega, the Beginning and the End. I will give of the fountain of the water of life freely to him who thirsts. He who overcomes shall inherit all things, and I will be his God, and he shall be My son."
Revelation21:6-7 NKJV

IT IS DONE! This is what God wanted all along: to dwell with His people, as a Father with His children, as a King with His beloved Bride. But watch that you are not found wanting.

"But the cowardly, unbelieving, abominable, murderers, sexually immoral, sorcerers, idolaters, and all liars shall have their part in the lake which burns with fire and brimstone, which is the second death.""

6. A River, a Tree, and an Invitation

"And he showed me a pure river of water of life, clear as crystal, proceeding from the throne of God and of the Lamb. In the middle of its street, and on either side of the river, was the tree of life, which bore twelve fruits, each tree yielding its fruit every month. The leaves of the tree were for the healing of the nations."
Revelation 22:1-2 NKJV

The story ends as it began—but greater. The tree that was guarded in Eden is now freely accessible. The curse is gone. The throne of God and of the Lamb is there. His servants see His face.

"And there shall be no more curse, but the throne of God and of the Lamb shall be in it, and His servants shall serve Him. They shall see His face, and His name shall be on their foreheads. There shall be no night there: They need no lamp nor light of the sun, for the Lord God gives them light. And they shall reign forever and ever."
Revelation 22:3-5 NKJV

And even in the final words, the invitation still stands:

"While it is said: "Today, if you will hear His voice, do not harden your hearts as in the rebellion.""
Hebrews 3:15 NKJV

"Again, He designates a certain day, saying in David, "Today," after such a long time, as it has been said: "Today, if you will hear His voice, do not harden your hearts.""
Hebrews 4:7 NKJV

"Behold, I stand at the door and knock. If anyone hears My voice and opens the door, I will come in to him and dine with him, and he with Me."
Revelation 3:20 NKJV

*"Come to Me, all you who labor and are heavy laden, and I will give
you rest."*
Matthew 11:28 NKJV

*"Repent therefore and be converted, that your sins may be blotted out,
so that times of refreshing may come from the presence of the Lord,"*
Acts 3:19 NKJV

*"On the last day, that great day of the feast, Jesus stood and cried out,
saying, "If anyone thirsts, let him come to Me and drink."*
John 7:37 NKJV

*""For behold, I create new heavens and a new earth; And the former
shall not be remembered or come to mind."*
Isaiah 65:17 NKJV

*"For there is no distinction between Jew and Greek, for the same Lord
over all is rich to all who call upon Him. For "whoever calls on the
name of the Lord shall be saved.""*
Romans 10:12-13 NKJV

*"And the Spirit and the bride say, "Come!" And let him who hears say,
"Come!" And let him who thirsts come. Whoever desires, let him take
the water of life freely.*
Revelation 22:17

*He who testifies to these things says, "Surely I am coming quickly."
Amen. Even so, come, Lord Jesus! The grace of our Lord Jesus Christ
be with you all. Amen."*
Revelation 22:20-21 NKJV

Conclusion: The End is the Beginning

This is not the end of the story. This is the beginning of what was
always meant to be.

"Declaring the end from the beginning, and from ancient times things

that are not yet done, Saying, 'My counsel shall stand, And I will do all
My pleasure,'"
Isaiah 46:10 NKJV

A world with no more pain.
A King who never leaves.
A city that never fades.
A people made pure, eternal, beloved.
A God who dwells with us—forever.

Let every heart prepare. Let every knee bow. Let every soul cry:

"Even so, come, Lord Jesus!"
(Revelation 22:20)

Final Prayer

O Sovereign Lord, Ancient of Days,

We humble ourselves before You, the One who declares the end from the beginning.

You are the God who sits above the circle of the earth,

Who raises up kings and casts them down,

Who rules over empires and humbles the proud.

Lord, we thank You for the light of Your Word—

for the revelation You have given through the prophets, through Your Son,

and through the Holy Spirit, who leads us into all truth.

We confess, Father, that we have often been dull of hearing,

slow to perceive and distracted by the kingdoms of this world.

But now, with unveiled eyes, we see the signs.

We hear the cry of the Bridegroom.

We discern the spirit of Babylon, and we reject it.

O God, awaken Your Church.

Strengthen every heart that reads these words.

Let no soul be deceived by the harlot, the beast, or the dragon.

Seal us with the name of the Lamb,

that we may endure to the end and not shrink back in the day of His coming.

Purify Your Bride, O Lord.

Make us watchful, faithful, and unashamed.

May we walk in holiness, in truth, and in the power of Your Spirit.

We long for the city whose builder and maker is God.

We await the return of the King of kings.

We cry out with the Spirit and the Bride:

"Come, Lord Jesus!"

Amen.

APPENDICES

Appendix A: The Meaning of "Babylon" in Hebrew

The Hebrew word for Babylon is לְכָב (Babel), which means "confusion" or "gateway of god."

This name originated in Genesis 11 during the rebellion at the Tower of Babel. Though humanity intended to create unity, they ended up with dispersion and confusion. This set the prophetic and spiritual tone for what would become a world system opposing God—Babylon.

Babylon in Scripture is more than a physical empire. It is a spiritual symbol of rebellion, idolatry, and worldliness. From Genesis to Revelation, Babylon is consistently shown as the embodiment of man's pride and religious deception.

Appendix B: Timeline of the Empires That Ruled Jerusalem

Daniel 2 Image	Daniel 7 Beast	Daniel 8 Vision	Historical Empire
Head of Gold	Lion	—	Babylon

Daniel 2 Image	Daniel 7 Beast	Daniel 8 Vision	Historical Empire
Chest & Arms	Bear	Ram	Persia
Belly & Thighs	Leopard	Goat	Greece
Legs of Iron	Dreadful beast	—	Roman Empire
Feet of Iron & Clay	10 Horns (on beast)	—	Modern Nations (10

All these empires played a role in dominating Jerusalem and fulfilling prophecy concerning Israel.

Appendix C: The Seventy-Year Servitude and Exile of Judah

Jeremiah 25:11–12 and Daniel 9:2 describe the 70-year servitude of Judah under Babylon. This exile was punishment for national disobedience, particularly the failure to keep the sabbath years (Leviticus 26:34–35).

God allowed the Babylonians to conquer Judah as judgment, but also as a prophetic time marker. This period leads directly into the prophecies of Daniel and into the Revelation of Jesus Christ.

Appendix D: Map of the Tribes of Israel and Their Scattering

- Northern Kingdom (Israel): Taken by Assyria (2 Kings 17:6) and scattered throughout the Assyrian empire.

- Southern Kingdom (Judah): Taken by Babylon (2 Kings 25), resulting in the 70-year exile.

Modern theories suggest remnants of the lost tribes migrated across Asia, Africa, and parts of Europe. Some claim tribal links in:

- Ethiopia (Dan)

- India (Manasseh)

- Afghanistan (Benjamin)

- West Africa (Judah/Levi)

While these theories are still debated, the scattering fulfilled Deuteronomy 28:64 and Amos 9:9.

Appendix E: Daniel's Visions Compared to Nebuchadnezzar's Dream

Daniel 2	Daniel 7	Daniel 8	Revelation 13 & 17
Gold (Babylon)	Lion	—	Dragon with crown
Silver (Persia)	Bear	Ram	Beast with 10 horns
Bronze (Greece)	Leopard	Goat	Beast like leopard
Iron (Rome)	Dreadful Beast	—	7 Heads, 10 Horns
Iron/Clay	Ten Horns/Beast	Beast	

Daniel 8 gives more detail on the conflict between Greece and Persia, with prophetic references to Alexander the Great and the rise of the Antichrist figure.

Appendix F: The Identity of the Little Horn

The Little Horn appears in both Daniel 7 and Daniel 8, but with distinctions:

- In Daniel 7: Rises among 10 horns, speaks blasphemies, and persecutes saints.

- In Daniel 8: Rises from one of the four horns (Greece), magnifies itself, casts down truth.

These are prophetic types:

Antiochus Epiphanes foreshadows the final Antichrist.

The final little horn arises out of a revived Roman system with global influence.

Appendix G: Understanding the Word "Church"

The Greek word ἐκκλησία (ekklesia) means "called-out ones."

- It refers to the body of believers, not a building or institution.

- It is not a translation of the Hebrew synagogue or temple.

The true Church was birthed at Pentecost (Acts 2), not during the Old Testament period, and it is distinct from Israel. It is built on Christ alone, not priests or human hierarchy.

Appendix H: Baptism by Immersion

The word baptism comes from the Greek βαπτίζω (baptizō), meaning "to immerse or submerge."

Scriptural support:

- Romans 6:3–4 — baptism is burial and resurrection.

- Acts 8:36–38 — Philip and the eunuch went down into the water.

Sprinkling or infant baptism is not biblical baptism.

Appendix I: Roles in the True Church

Ephesians 4:11 defines five roles:

- Apostles

- Prophets

- Evangelists

- Pastors

- Teachers

Nowhere does Scripture refer to "popes," "priests," or "fathers" as ruling offices in the Church. Jesus said in Matthew 23:9, "Do not call anyone on earth your father; for One is your Father, He who is in heaven."

Appendix J: The Identity of Mystery Babylon

Mystery Babylon is not ancient Babylon—it is a spiritual system revealed in Revelation 17–18.

Identifying traits:

A woman, arrayed in purple and scarlet (17:4)

Holds a golden cup (religious symbol)

Sits on seven hills (17:9)

Rules over kings (17:18)

Drunk with the blood of saints (17:6)

These attributes align closely with the Roman Catholic Church, its location, wealth, political power, and history of persecuting true believers.

Appendix K: The Two Women of Revelation

Description	Revelation 12 (Woman Clothed in Sun)	Revelation 17 (Mystery Babylon)
Symbol	Israel/Church	False Religion
Location	Heaven	Wilderness
Apparel	Sun, Moon, Stars	Purple, Scarlet, Gold
Outcome	Persecuted but preserved	Judged and destroyed
Offspring	Jesus Christ and true believers	Harlots and abominations

This contrast highlights the true Bride and the apostate harlot.

Appendix L: The Beast from the Earth (Revelation 13:11)

This second beast appears as a lamb but speaks like a dragon.

- Exercises all the authority of the first beast.

- Performs false miracles.

- Causes the world to worship the first beast.

This is the False Prophet, who symbolizes false religion. The papal system, claiming divine titles and deceiving the world, fits this prophetic image.

Appendix M: Seven Heads and Ten Horns

Feature	Revelation 12	Revelation 13	Revelation 17
Heads	7 (with 7 diadems)	7 (with blasphemies)	7 kings/mountains
Horns	10 (no crowns)	10 (with crowns)	10 kings (end-time)

- The 7 heads are religious-political powers—papal succession.

- The 10 horns are modern nations giving authority to the beast in the end-time global system.

Appendix N: End-Times Chronology

1. The snatching of the Church (harpazō)

2. Rise of the Antichrist

3. Seven-year tribulation

4. Seals, trumpets, and bowl judgments

5. Armageddon and return of Jesus

6. 1000-year reign of Christ

7. Final judgment and new creation

This sequence aligns Daniel's weeks with Revelation's unfolding prophecy.

Appendix O: Understanding the Word "Rapture"

The term rapture comes from the Latin raptura, translating the Greek ἁρπάζω (harpazō) — "to snatch suddenly."

Key texts:

- 1 Thessalonians 4:16–17

- 1 Corinthians 15:52

The event is certain, but the timing is debated. This book does not use Catholic eschatology but seeks clarity from the Word alone.

- The 7 heads are religious-political powers—papal succession.

- The 10 horns are modern nations giving authority to the beast in the end-time global system.

Appendix N: End-Times Chronology

1. The rise of the Antichrist

2. The snatching of the church

3. Seven-year tribulation

4. Seals, trumpets, and bowl judgments

5. Armageddon and return of Jesus

6. 1000-year reign of Christ

7. Final judgment and new creation

This sequence aligns Daniel's weeks with Revelation's unfolding prophecy.

Appendix O: Understanding the Word "Rapture"

The term rapture comes from the Latin raptura, translating the Greek ἁρπάζω (harpazō) — "to snatch suddenly."

Key texts:

- 1 Thessalonians 4:16–17

- 1 Corinthians 15:52

The event is certain, but the timing is debated. This book does not use

Roman Catholic Church eschatology but seeks clarity from the Word alone.

Appendix P: Prophetic Symbols and Their Meanings

Symbol	Meaning	Reference
Beast	Empire or King	Daniel 7:17, Revelation 13
Horn	Kingdom or King	Daniel 8:21, Revelation 17
Woman	Religious system	Revelation 12 & 17
Stars	Angels or leaders	Revelation 1:20
Water	Multitudes and nations	Revelation 17:15
Mountain	Kingdom	Daniel 2:35, Revelation 17
Lamb	Jesus Christ	John 1:29, Revelation 5:6
Dragon	Satan	Revelation 12:9

These symbols help decode the rich prophetic language of Daniel and Revelation.

About the Author

Peter Lengwe is a devoted student of biblical prophecy and theology with a passion for unveiling the deep truths of Scripture. His writing is marked by reverence for the Word of God, a commitment to sound doctrine, and a desire to awaken the Church to the times we are living in.

His first book, In the Beginning: The Heavens and the Earth as Created, explored the divine foundation of the world from a biblical creationist perspective. His second work, Pierced for Our Transgressions, took readers on a powerful devotional and doctrinal journey through the final days of Jesus Christ, aligning the Gospel narrative with the Hebrew calendar and prophetic fulfillment.

In this third volume, Mystery Babylon and World Beasts Unveiled, Peter leads readers into the prophetic heart of God's dealings with nations—from the rise of Babel to the coming judgment of the final beast. Drawing deeply from the books of Daniel, Revelation, and the prophetic timeline of Scripture, he offers a Spirit-led guide through the mysteries that have confounded scholars and saints alike.

Peter writes not as a theologian behind a pulpit, but as a watchman on the wall—calling the faithful to discern the signs of the times, return to the truth of Scripture, and live ready for the return of the King.

www.ingramcontent.com/pod-product-compliance
Lightning Source LLC
Chambersburg PA
CBHW051208160726
47994CB00002B/512

9 781972 299661